ADULTING 101:
LIFE SKILLS FOR YOUNG ADULTS

Learn How to Manage Your Money Responsibly, Communicate More Effectively and Balance Work-Life Happiness for GEN-Z

SAM MATTHEWS

TABLE OF CONTENTS

Introduction	9
1. Financial Foundations for Independence	11
1.1 Crafting a Realistic Budget for Your Lifestyle	11
1.2 Understanding Credit Scores and Building Credit	13
1.3 Debt Management: Avoiding Pitfalls and Building Resilience	15
1.4 Savings Strategies: For Short and Long-Term Goals	17
1.5 Demystifying Taxes: What You Need to Know	19
1.6 Financial Tools and Apps That Simplify Your Life	21
2. Communication Skills for Personal and Professional Success	23
2.1 Active Listening: The Key to Understanding and Connection	25
2.2 Conflict Resolution: Navigating Difficult Conversations	27
2.3 Public Speaking Skills: Confidence in Front of an Audience	29
2.4 Networking 101: Building Authentic Professional Relationships	31
2.5 Social Media Savvy: Communicating Effectively Online	33
3. Navigating the Workplace: Career Development and Success	35
3.1 Sample Resume and Cover Letter	37
3.2 Acing the Job Interview: Practical Tips and Tricks	39

3.3 Building Your Personal Brand: LinkedIn and Beyond	41
3.4 Navigating Workplace Dynamics and Politics	43
3.5 Continuous Learning: Upskilling for Career Growth	45
3.6 Understanding Employment Benefits: Making the Most of Your Package	47
4. Time Management and a Healthy Work-Life Balance	**50**
4.1 Setting Boundaries: Protecting Your Personal Time	53
4.2 Creating a Flexible Schedule That Works for You	54
4.3 Digital Detox: Balancing Screen Time and Personal Life	56
4.4 Self-Care Routines for a Balanced Life	58
4.5 Mindfulness Practices for Stress Reduction	60
5. Mastering the Basics: Cooking, Nutrition, and Home Skills	**64**
5.1 Meal Planning on a Budget: Eating Healthy Without Breaking the Bank	67
5.2 Understanding Nutrition Labels: Making Informed Choices	68
5.3 Essential Kitchen Skills: From Boiling to Baking	69
5.4 Basic Home Repairs Everyone Should Know	71
5.5 Cleaning Hacks: For a Tidy, Stress-Free Environment	74
6. Digital Literacy and Online Safety	**77**

6.1 Data Privacy: Protecting Your Personal Information	79
6.2 Recognizing and Avoiding Online Scams	81
6.3 Cybersecurity Basics: Keeping Your Devices Safe	82
6.4 Social Media Best Practices: Sharing Smartly and Safely	84
6.5 Digital Well-Being: Balancing Online and Offline Life	86
7. Building Emotional Intelligence (EI) and Mental Resilience	**88**
7.1 Stress Management Techniques for Everyday Life	91
7.2 Building Resilience: Bouncing Back from Setbacks	93
7.3 Cultivating a Growth Mindset: Embracing Challenges.	95
7.4 Establishing a Support Network: The Power of Community	97
7.5 Seeking Professional Help: When and How to Reach Out	99
8. Creating a Fulfilling and Purposeful Life	**101**
8.1 Pursuing Passions and Hobbies: Enriching Your Life	103
8.2 Sustainable Living: Making Eco-Friendly Choices.	105
8.3 Volunteering and Giving Back: Creating Impactful Change.	107
8.4 Maintaining Healthy Relationships: Communication and Boundaries	109
8.5 Embracing Change and Uncertainty with Confidence	111

CONCLUSION	113
REFERENCES	116

DEDICATION

This book is dedicated to my two wonderful sons who made being a good dad easy. ☺

INTRODUCTION

Some years ago, I found myself standing in the middle of my first apartment, surrounded by a sea of boxes. The excitement of having my own space was mixed with a wave of anxiety. How would I handle bills, clean the place, and manage my time? These questions were daunting, but they were part of the journey into adulthood that we all face.

This book is here to guide you through these challenges and more. It's a roadmap designed to help you gain the skills needed to thrive as an independent adult. We'll cover everything from managing your money wisely to communicating effectively and balancing work with life happiness. This guide will be your 'Go-To' companion if you're stepping into adult responsibilities.

Who is this book for? It's for young adults, particularly those from Gen-Z, who are stepping into adult responsibilities. Whether you're starting your first full-time job, moving out on your own, or just looking to make sense of adult life, this book is for you. We focus on building the skills that matter most as you navigate this exciting chapter of your life.

We'll explore several core themes throughout the book. Financial literacy is critical, so we'll dive into budgeting, saving, and smart spending. Communication skills are also crucial, whether you're in a job interview or negotiating with a roommate. Work-life balance is another big theme, as finding time for career and personal life can be tricky. We will also look at digital literacy, mental well-being, and personal growth to round out your skills to succeed.

My journey through adulthood has given me insights I want to share with you. I've seen the struggles and triumphs of young adults as they step into independence. I have a deep passion for helping you overcome these challenges and find success. This book is a product of that passion and a desire to see you thrive.

What can you expect in the chapters ahead? We'll provide practical advice and real-life examples to clarify each concept. You'll find interactive elements like quizzes and exercises to help you apply what you learn. Each chapter is crafted to engage and educate, making complex ideas simple and actionable.

I hope you experience a transformation by the end of this book. You'll feel more confident and ready to tackle the challenges of adult life, and the skills you develop will empower you to handle responsibilities with enthusiasm and poise.

As you read, I encourage you to engage actively with the content. Take notes, jot down your thoughts, and apply the advice to your life. Each page offers an opportunity for self-discovery and growth.

So, let's dive in. Together, we'll navigate this path of adulthood with confidence and curiosity. The adventure is yours, and it starts now.

Chapter 1

Financial Foundations for Independence

Stepping into adulthood often feels like standing at the edge of a vast ocean, ready to set sail without a map. One of the first waves to hit is managing finances independently. I remember the first time I tried to figure out a budget. I stood at my kitchen table, surrounded by bills and receipts, feeling overwhelmed. The moment made me realize how much I needed a plan. You might be feeling the same way about your finances. This chapter is about giving you the tools to create that map and confidently navigate the waters of personal finance. We'll cover the essentials of budgeting, a skill that forms the bedrock of your financial independence. Understanding how to budget effectively is crucial, as it provides a clear picture of your financial health and sets the stage for achieving your goals. Let's dive into the nitty-gritty details of crafting a realistic budget tailored just for you.

1.1 Crafting a Realistic Budget for Your Lifestyle

Budgeting is more than just a spreadsheet or a list of numbers; it's about setting boundaries that allow you to live comfortably while planning for the future. The importance of a budget cannot be overstated. It is the foundation of financial health, helping you understand where your money goes and how to control it. This framework is your guide to making informed decisions, ensuring you're not just living paycheck to paycheck but actually saving and preparing for what lies ahead. Begin with a simple template that lists your income sources and expenses. You'll want to categorize expenses into fixed, variable, and discretionary. Fixed Expenses are those regular, unchanging costs like rent or a car payment. Variable Expenses can fluctuate, such as groceries, utility bills, or the price of gasoline. Discretionary Spending includes those little extras, like dining out or entertainment. By identifying these, you can see where adjustments might be made.

Once you have a clear view of your financial landscape, it's time to set up your personal budget. Start by tracking your income and expenses meticulously. Use a notebook, a spreadsheet, or a budgeting app to record every dollar coming in and going out. This might seem tedious at first, but it provides invaluable insight into your financial habits. Setting financial goals is the next step. Whether paying off student loans, saving for a vacation, or building an emergency fund, having clear objectives will guide your budgeting decisions. Break down your goals into achievable steps, and monitor your progress regularly to stay motivated.

Budgeting isn't just about numbers; it's about mindset. Many people face psychological barriers when it comes to managing their money. Budget fatigue is real and it can happen when you feel constrained by your financial plan. To avoid this, remember to be flexible. Adjust your budget as your circumstances change, and don't be afraid to tweak it if you find certain areas too restrictive. Impulse spending is another common challenge. It can derail even the best-laid plans. Combat this by setting aside a small amount for spontaneous purchases, allowing yourself to enjoy life's little pleasures without guilt.

To stick to your budget, consider using tools and techniques that simplify the process. The envelope budgeting method is a classic approach where you allocate a specific amount of cash to different spending categories, keeping it in labeled envelopes. This tactile method helps you visualize your spending limits. But this is an old technique. Today, budgeting apps can be incredibly helpful on the digital front. YNAB (You Need A Budget) is highly recommended for its goal-setting features and proactive budgeting approach. For those who prefer a more straightforward method, Goodbudget offers an excellent digital version of the envelope system with both free and paid options (SOURCE 1). These tools organize your finances and provide insights into your spending patterns, helping you make better decisions.

Crafting a budget is an ongoing process that requires regular review and adjustment. It's about creating a system that works for you and supports your lifestyle, not the other way around. As you refine your budgeting skills, you'll find that financial independence is not just a concept but a tangible reality within your reach.

1.2 Understanding Credit Scores and Building Credit

Navigating the world of credit can feel like deciphering a complex code, yet understanding it is key to unlocking many opportunities in adulthood. A credit score is a three-digit number that tells lenders about your reliability as a borrower. It's built from several components, the most significant being your payment history. This makes up about 35% of your score and reflects how well you've paid your bills in the past. Late payments can knock points off your score and signal to lenders that you might not be reliable. Another critical factor is the credit utilization ratio, which constitutes 30% of your score. This measures how much of your available credit you're using. Ideally, you should aim to use less than 30% of your credit limit. High usage indicates financial stress to lenders, even if you're not actually struggling, and can lower your score. Understanding these components helps clarify why maintaining good credit habits is crucial.

Credit Score Ranges

- Excellent: 800–850
- Very good: 740–799
- Good: 670–739
- Fair: 580–669
- Poor: 300–579

Building and improving your credit might seem daunting, but it's all about forming smart habits. If you're new to credit or looking to boost your score, consider starting with a secured credit card. These cards require a deposit that serves as your credit limit, making them a low-risk way to build credit. For example, the Discover it® Secured Credit Card offers cash back on purchases and no annual fee, making it a good starting point for those new to credit (SOURCE 2). Once you have a card, use it responsibly. Pay off your balance in full each month to avoid interest charges and keep your utilization low. Set up automatic payments to ensure you're never late. Your credit score will improve as you demonstrate good habits, opening doors to better financial products with favorable terms.

Ignoring credit can have long-lasting repercussions. A low credit score can lead to higher interest rates on loans or even being denied credit altogether. This makes big purchases, like buying a car or a house, more expensive in the long run. Renting an apartment can also become challenging, as landlords often check credit scores as part of their application process. A low score might signal financial irresponsibility, leading them to choose another applicant over you. These consequences highlight the importance of actively managing your credit rather than letting it fall by the wayside.

Monitoring your credit report regularly is essential to maintain your financial health. You're entitled to a free credit report annually from each of the three major credit bureaus—Equifax, Experian, and TransUnion. Use AnnualCreditReport.com to access these reports and review them for any inaccuracies. If you spot an error, such as an incorrect late payment or a misreported account, dispute it immediately. Contact the credit bureau in question, provide documentation to support your claim, and follow up until it's resolved. Correcting these errors can significantly impact your credit score, ensuring it accurately reflects your creditworthiness.

1.3 Debt Management:

Avoiding Pitfalls and Building Resilience

Debt can feel like a shadow, always lurking in the background of your financial life, but understanding it is the first step to managing it effectively. Let's start by distinguishing the good from the bad. Good debt is typically an investment in your future, like student loans or a mortgage that offers a return over time. Student loans, for instance, can be considered good debt if they lead to a degree and better job prospects. They often come with lower interest rates and flexible repayment plans. On the flip side, credit card debt usually falls into the bad debt category. It's easy to accumulate due to high interest rates and the temptation of easy spending. This type of debt can quickly spiral out of control, leading to significant financial strain. Recognizing these differences helps you prioritize which debts to tackle first and underscores the importance of strategic repayment.

Managing and reducing debt requires a plan. Two popular methods are the debt snowball and debt avalanche approaches. The snowball method focuses on paying off the smallest debts first, providing quick wins and motivation to tackle larger ones. You pay the minimum on all but the smallest debt, which you attack aggressively until it's gone. This approach is excellent for building momentum. The avalanche method, however, targets debts with the highest interest rates first, reducing the overall amount paid over time. This can save more money eventually but may feel slower because the highest-interest debts are often the largest. Both strategies have merits, and choosing one depends on your financial situation and psychological preferences. Debt consolidation loans can also help by combining multiple debts into one loan with a lower interest rate, simplifying payments and potentially reducing costs.

Resilience in debt management is vital. Financial resilience is about maintaining your financial health even when burdened by debt. Building an emergency fund is a key component. This fund acts as a safety net, preventing you from falling back into debt when unexpected expenses arise. Start small, aiming to save enough to cover a month of expenses, then gradually increase it. Alongside this, create a debt repayment plan. Outline your debts, prioritize them, and set a timeline for repayment. This plan provides structure and helps maintain focus and motivation, even when progress feels slow.

Consider the story of a friend who found himself drowning in credit card debt after college. On almost every college campus, banks and credit card companies offer free tee shirts and other tokens if you sign up for their credit card. It's easy to fall for their offering and even easier to use those credit cards to make unnecessary purchases. My friend felt overwhelmed by his poor decision-making but decided to take control using the debt snowball method. He gradually chipped away at his debt by paying off one card at a time. Each paid-off card was a victory, boosting his confidence! He complemented this with a small emergency fund, which kept him from relying on credit cards again when something like unexpected car repairs came up. Over time, he cleared his debt entirely, and the relief was palpable. This success wasn't just about removing a financial burden; it was about reclaiming control of his financial life and building resilience for the future.

Debt management isn't just about numbers; it's about fostering a mindset of resilience and control. By understanding your debt, choosing a repayment strategy, and building a safety net, you lay the groundwork for financial stability. This isn't an overnight fix, but with persistence and a clear plan, the weight of debt can be lifted, giving way to financial freedom.

1.4 Savings Strategies:

For Short and Long-Term Goals

Saving money can feel like trying to fill a bucket with a hole at the bottom. Every time you think you're making progress, an unexpected expense appears, setting you back. Yet, saving is one of the most important habits you can develop for financial security. It's essential—not just for buying the things you want but for creating a safety net that shields you from life's unpredictability. One of the first things you should consider is building an emergency fund. This fund acts as your financial safety net, covering unexpected expenses like medical bills or car repairs without derailing your finances. Experts often suggest having three to six months' worth of living expenses saved up. It might sound daunting, but starting small, even with just a few dollars a week, can make a significant difference over time. On the other hand, planning for retirement might seem like a distant concern, but starting early is crucial. The power of compound interest means that the earlier you save, the more benefits you will see over time.

Various strategies can help you save effectively. One popular method is the 50/30/20 rule. According to this rule, you allocate 50% of your income to necessities like rent and groceries, 30% to discretionary spending like entertainment, and 20% to savings and debt repayment. This straightforward approach helps balance immediate needs with future goals. Additionally, consider high-yield savings accounts, which offer higher interest rates than traditional ones. These accounts can significantly boost your savings, with some offering rates exceeding 4%, such as those highlighted in Forbes' analysis of high-yield savings accounts (SOURCE 4). By placing your savings in an account that works for you, you're ensuring your money grows even while it sits idle.

Automating your savings is another powerful tool to ensure consistency. You can automatically transfer a portion of your paycheck into your savings account by setting up direct deposit. This method removes the need for manual transfers and helps you stick to your savings goals without thinking about it. Automation makes saving a default behavior, reducing the temptation to spend that money elsewhere. With direct deposit, you're essentially paying yourself first, which is a critical mindset for successful saving. It's like setting your financial goals on autopilot, allowing you to focus on other aspects of your life.

Setting and achieving savings goals requires intention and planning. Using the SMART goal framework—Specific, Measurable, Achievable, Relevant, and Time-bound—can help you set clear, realistic targets. For example, instead of saying, "I want to save money," specify, "I want to save $1,000 for a vacation by next summer." This goal is specific (saving $1,000), measurable (you can track progress), achievable (consider your income and expenses), relevant (aligns with personal desires), and time-bound (by next summer). This clarity transforms vague intentions into concrete plans, increasing the likelihood of success. Regularly reviewing and adjusting these goals ensures they align with your financial situation and personal priorities.

To visualize your progress and stay motivated:

1. Consider creating a savings chart.
2. Place it somewhere visible, like on your fridge or desk, and update it regularly as you reach your milestones. This tangible representation of your progress can be a powerful motivator, reminding you of your goals and celebrating each step forward.
3. Remember, saving is not about depriving yourself but creating opportunities and security.

It's all about making informed choices that lead to a more stable and fulfilling life. By adopting these strategies, you set yourself up for financial success and peace of mind, knowing you have a plan in place for both the expected and the unexpected.

A personal example of looking ahead: I set up a 529 College Fund account for my sons when they were born. It was not a lot of money each month, but an amount I didn't notice was missing from my pay. As my salary increased, I increased the monthly deposits. By the time they graduated from High School, we had enough money saved to pay for most of their college expenses. It's not small feets, but it's very doable.

1.5 Demystifying Taxes: What You Need to Know

Taxes can feel like a maze, especially when you're just starting out on your own. But understanding them is crucial—it's a rite of passage into adulthood. Let's start with the basics. Every year, by April 15th, millions of Americans file their taxes, and among the crucial documents involved is the W-2 form. This form is a summary from your employer detailing how much you earned and how much was withheld for taxes throughout the year. Your W-2 is pivotal because it provides the information needed to file your tax return accurately. Filing on time is equally important. Missing the deadline can result in penalties and interest on any taxes owed.

Think of it like returning a library book late—the longer you wait, the more you pay. By submitting your return promptly, you avoid unnecessary fees and ensure you're eligible for any refund due.

Once you're familiar with the W-2 and the importance of timely filing, it's time to explore deductions and credits—two powerful tools that can reduce your taxable income and increase your refund. For young adults, education credits are particularly relevant. Suppose you're paying for college tuition or repaying student loans. In that case, you might qualify for the American Opportunity Credit or the Lifetime Learning Credit. These credits can significantly lower your tax bill. Additionally, the interest paid on student loans is often deductible, easing the financial burden. Understanding these benefits is like finding hidden treasure in the tax code; it means more money to use as you see fit.

There's a lot of misinformation floating around about taxes, and it's essential to set the record straight. For instance, tax brackets are often misunderstood. Many believe earning more will push them into a higher bracket, resulting in more taxes on their income. This is a myth. In reality, only the income above each bracket's threshold is taxed at a higher rate, while the rest remains taxed at lower rates. It's a progressive system designed to be fair but often misinterpreted. Clarifying these misconceptions allows you to approach tax planning with confidence, knowing that a raise or bonus won't penalize your entire earnings.

Navigating taxes doesn't have to be a solo endeavor. Numerous resources are available to help you along the way. Free tax filing software, such as TurboTax Free Edition or H&R Block Free Online, offers step-by-step guidance through the filing process, making it accessible even if you're a novice. If you prefer a more hands-on approach, the IRS provides a wealth of resources on its website, including interactive tools and FAQs. For those with more complex tax situations, seeking assistance from a certified tax professional can be invaluable. They can offer tailored advice and ensure you take advantage of every possible deduction and credit. Remember, taxes require patience and attention to detail, like assembling a puzzle, but you can fit all the pieces together with the right resources.

1.6 Financial Tools and Apps That Simplify Your Life

In today's fast-paced world, managing your finances can feel like juggling too many balls at once. Luckily, technology offers tools to make this task more manageable. Financial apps and platforms simplify the process, helping you gain better control over your money. Budgeting apps like YNAB (You Need A Budget) offer features that help track expenses and set financial goals. These apps often come with handy notifications, reminding you to stay within your budget and avoid overspending. Investment platforms like Acorns and Robinhood open the door to investing, even if you're just starting out. Acorns round up your purchases to the nearest dollar and invest the spare change, making it easy to dip your toes into investing without needing a large sum of money. On the other hand, Robinhood provides a platform for trading stocks without commission fees, making it appealing to those who want more control over their investments. These tools are designed to fit seamlessly into your life, guiding you toward smarter financial decisions.

Using technology to manage finances brings numerous benefits. With real-time expense tracking, you get an immediate snapshot of your spending habits, allowing you to adjust and make informed decisions. This immediate feedback is like having a financial advisor in your pocket, nudging you toward healthier financial habits. Additionally, many apps offer automated savings features. You can set up rules that automatically transfer small amounts into savings accounts, making saving money effortless. This automation ensures you consistently set aside funds, turning saving into a painless habit rather than a chore. The integration of technology into financial management streamlines the process and enhances financial literacy, making complicated concepts easy to understand.

However, relying solely on digital tools does have its drawbacks. Privacy is a significant concern, as these apps require access to sensitive financial information. It's crucial to ensure any app you choose uses robust security measures to protect your data. Additionally, there's the risk of becoming too dependent on technology. If you're not careful, you might find yourself lost if an app suddenly becomes unavailable or changes its terms of service. Maintaining a basic understanding of your finances outside these tools is essential, as well as using them as aids rather than crutches. Balancing technology with personal knowledge creates a more resilient financial management strategy.

When choosing the right financial tools, consider your lifestyle and financial goals. Evaluate each app's features—do they offer the support and capabilities you need? User reviews and recommendations can provide insight into an app's reliability and user-friendliness. Look for apps with a track record of excellent customer service and frequent updates, which indicate a commitment to improving user experience. Cost is another factor; some apps offer free versions with limited features, while others require a subscription for full access. Make sure the benefits align with what you're willing to spend. Ultimately, the right tool should feel intuitive and enhance your financial management, not complicate it.

These tools will likely become more integrated into daily life as technology evolves. They provide a window into your financial world, offering insights that were once difficult to obtain. While they can't replace the value of understanding your finances personally, they serve as valuable aids. By embracing these resources, you can gain greater control over your financial health, setting the stage for a stable and prosperous future. As you explore these options, remember that the best tool is one that aligns with your personal goals and lifestyle, helping you navigate the complexities of financial life with confidence and ease.

Chapter 2

Communication Skills for Personal and Professional Success

Picture this: you've just landed your first job, and the excitement is overwhelming. You're eager to make a great impression and show them what you've got. But then, an email in your inbox requests a detailed report by the end of the week. Suddenly, the thrill of your new role is tinged with a bit of anxiety. How do you respond professionally, ensuring clarity and respect while showcasing your competence? This scenario is all too familiar for many young adults stepping into the workforce. Navigating the world of professional communication, especially email, can be tricky. However, mastering it can set you apart and pave the way for success.

Emails are a cornerstone of professional communication. They serve as a record of conversations and are often the first impression colleagues and superiors will have of your communication skills. A well-structured email starts with a compelling subject line. This is like the headline of an article, grabbing attention and providing insight into the content. It should be concise yet informative, giving the recipient a reason to open the email immediately. If you're requesting feedback on a project, a subject line like "Request for Feedback on Project XYZ by Friday" is clear and to the point. Once the subject line has drawn them in, proper salutations and closings frame your message with professionalism. Begin with a respectful greeting tailored to your relationship with the recipient. "Dear [Name]" or "Hello [Name]" are often safe bets. In the end, a courteous closing such as "Best regards" or "Thank you" leaves a positive impression, wrapping up the communication neatly.

The tone and clarity of your email can make or break its effectiveness. Emails should be clear and respectful, avoiding jargon and ambiguous phrases that could lead to misunderstandings. Consider your audience's knowledge and familiarity with the topic when crafting your message. If you're writing to a technical team about a software update, ensure your language is precise and free from technical jargon that others might not understand. Instead of saying, "Let's expedite the deployment of the new feature," which might confuse some, try, "Could we prioritize launching the new feature by next Thursday?" This approach ensures that all understand your message, fostering better communication.

Proofreading is a crucial step that cannot be overlooked. It's your opportunity to catch and correct errors before hitting send. Common mistakes in grammar and spelling can undermine your professionalism, potentially altering the recipient's perception of your attention to detail. Reading your email aloud can help identify awkward phrasing or errors that your eyes might skip over. Additionally, consider using tools like Grammarly or Microsoft Word's spell-check to enhance accuracy. These tools offer suggestions for improving your writing, ensuring your message is polished and professional. A well-proofread email reflects the care and diligence you apply to your work, reinforcing your reliability and competence.

Managing email correspondence efficiently is another skill to hone. Given the high volume of emails exchanged daily, it's essential to prioritize and respond promptly. Set aside specific times during the day to check and respond to emails rather than letting your inbox dictate your workflow. This approach helps maintain focus on your tasks while ensuring important communications are addressed promptly. Categorize emails by urgency and importance to streamline your responses. For instance, tackle an email requiring a quick answer immediately. For more complex queries, consider flagging them for a dedicated time slot when you can give them the attention they deserve. This system keeps your inbox manageable and ensures that you remain responsive and efficient, which are highly valued qualities in any professional setting.

Email Etiquette Checklist

- Subject Line: Is it concise and informative?
- Greeting & Closing: Are they appropriate for the recipient?
- Tone & Clarity: Is it a clear message and free from jargon?
- Proofreading: Check for grammar and spelling errors?
- Response Time: Is my email prioritized and timely?

This checklist is a quick reference to ensure your emails meet professional standards. By incorporating these practices into your daily routine, you can transform your email communication from a mundane task into a powerful tool for career growth.

2.1 Active Listening:

The Key to Understanding and Connection

Imagine sitting in a crowded café, a friend across the table sharing an important story, but your mind drifts to the emails waiting for you at work. You nod occasionally, aware that you're hearing them speak but not truly listening. This scenario is common, yet it illustrates the crucial difference between hearing and listening. Hearing is passive; it's the physiological act of sound waves hitting your eardrums. Listening, however, is active. It involves processing, understanding, and responding to the information being shared. Engagement is the backbone of effective communication in personal or professional relationships.

To practice active listening, you need dedication and awareness. It starts with simple techniques like paraphrasing and summarizing. When someone shares their thoughts, try restating their ideas in your own words to confirm your understanding. For instance, if a colleague outlines a project plan, you might say, "So, you're suggesting we focus on the marketing strategy before finalizing the budget, right?" This shows that you're engaged and provides clarity for both parties. Non-verbal cues are equally important. Eye contact, nodding, and leaning slightly forward signal your attention and interest. Imagine a friend recounting a difficult experience; your attentive posture and occasional nods can convey empathy and support without uttering a single word.

Several barriers can hinder active listening, but they're not insurmountable. Distractions are a primary culprit. External noise can pull your focus away, whether it's the buzzing of your phone or the chatter of a nearby conversation. To counter this, create an environment conducive to listening. Silence notifications, find a quieter space, or inform the speaker if you need a moment to refocus. Preconceived notions also pose challenges. It's easy to listen with an agenda, filtering what you hear through biases or assumptions. To overcome this, approach each conversation with an open mind. Suspend judgments and allow the speaker to express themselves fully before forming conclusions. This openness paves the way for genuine understanding and connection.

The benefits of active listening extend far beyond mere comprehension. It fosters empathy, allowing you to step into another's shoes and see the world from their perspective. In personal relationships, this deepens connections, building trust and mutual respect. A friend who feels honestly heard is more likely to confide in you, strengthening your bond. In professional settings, active listening enhances collaboration and teamwork. Colleagues who practice it are better equipped to navigate complex projects, resolve misunderstandings, and innovate together. It becomes a foundation for constructive dialogue, where ideas flow freely, and solutions emerge organically.

Active listening is not just a skill; it's a mindset that can transform interactions and lead to stronger, more meaningful connections. It requires intention and practice but offers rewards that resonate in every facet of life. As you hone this ability, you'll find that the quality of your conversations improves, whether you're discussing weekend plans with a friend or strategizing with a team at work. The act of genuinely listening transforms communication from a mere exchange of words to a profound connection between people.

2.2 Conflict Resolution:

Navigating Difficult Conversations

We've all been stuck in a disagreement that seems impossible to navigate. Conflict is an inevitable part of life, especially when different perspectives and values collide. Often, misunderstandings arise from simple miscommunication, where the intended message gets lost in translation. Differing values can also spark disputes, as what is paramount to one person may hold little weight for another.

These conflicts can emerge in any setting, from the workplace to personal relationships, and knowing how to manage them is crucial for maintaining harmony and understanding.

To effectively resolve conflicts, it's helpful to have a toolkit of strategies at your disposal. One such tool is the "I" statement technique, which focuses on expressing your feelings and needs without assigning blame. Instead of saying, "You never listen to my ideas," reframe it as "I feel overlooked when my ideas aren't considered." This approach shifts the conversation from accusations to personal experiences, reducing defensiveness and opening the door for constructive dialogue. Finding common ground is another critical strategy. You can steer the conversation towards collaboration rather than confrontation by identifying shared goals or values. This might involve acknowledging the validity of the other person's perspective, even if you don't entirely agree, and working together to find a solution that satisfies both parties.

Emotional intelligence plays a pivotal role in resolving conflicts. Understanding and managing your emotional responses can prevent disputes from escalating. Feeling angry or frustrated during a disagreement is natural, but reacting impulsively can damage relationships. Instead, take a moment to breathe and assess your emotions before responding. This pause allows you to communicate more effectively and approach the situation with a clear mind. Recognizing the emotions of others is equally important. By showing empathy and acknowledging their feelings, you build trust and demonstrate that you value their perspective. This empathetic approach can diffuse tension and foster a more cooperative environment.

Consider a scenario where two colleagues clash over project responsibilities. Initially, both parties are frustrated, feeling that their contributions aren't being recognized. Using "I" statements, they express their concerns without placing blame. "I feel like my efforts aren't acknowledged, which makes me less motivated," one says. The other responds, "I understand and feel similarly about my role." Acknowledging each other's feelings, they find common ground in their shared desire for recognition. This mutual understanding paves the way for compromise, where they agree to rotate leadership roles on the project, ensuring both have opportunities to shine. This resolution addresses their immediate concerns and strengthens their working relationship, enhancing future collaboration.

Conflicts, when managed well, can lead to growth and stronger connections. Approaching them with a mindset of understanding and cooperation transforms them from divisive events into opportunities for learning and improvement. You can navigate difficult conversations with confidence and empathy by employing techniques like "I" statements, finding common ground, and cultivating emotional intelligence. Whether at work or in personal life, these skills are invaluable, helping you maintain healthy relationships and a positive environment.

2.3 Public Speaking Skills:

Confidence in Front of an Audience

Standing in front of an audience, whether a small group of colleagues or a packed auditorium, can be nerve-wracking. Yet, the ability to speak confidently and effectively in public is a powerful skill that opens doors in both personal and professional realms. The foundation of a successful speech lies in its structure. Think of your speech as a well-crafted story with a clear beginning, middle, and end. The introduction should grab attention, perhaps through an intriguing fact or a personal anecdote, setting the stage for what's to come. The body of your speech is where you delve into the core message, weaving in facts, examples, and personal insights to support your points. Conclude with a strong, memorable ending that reinforces your message and leaves the audience with a call to action or a thought-provoking idea.

Public speaking anxiety is a common hurdle, but it can be managed with practice and the proper techniques. Visualization exercises are particularly effective. Before your presentation, close your eyes and picture yourself delivering a flawless speech. Imagine the audience reacting positively, nodding in agreement, and applauding at the end. This mental rehearsal can boost your confidence and reduce anxiety. Breathing techniques also play a crucial role. Practice slow, deep breaths to calm your nerves and steady your voice. Inhale deeply through your nose, hold for a few seconds, then exhale slowly. This simple exercise helps control the physiological symptoms of anxiety, like trembling or a racing heart, allowing you to focus on delivering your message.

Body language and vocal variety are key elements of engaging public speaking. Your non-verbal cues can convey confidence, enthusiasm, and authority. Use gestures to emphasize points, but ensure they are natural and not distracting. For instance, a sweeping hand gesture can highlight a critical moment, while a firm stance with eye contact can convey confidence. Similarly, vocal variety keeps your audience engaged. Vary your pitch, pace, and volume to emphasize different parts of your speech. A pause can be powerful, giving your audience a moment to absorb your message. By adjusting your voice and using body language effectively, you can maintain interest and ensure your message resonates with your audience.

Practice and feedback are invaluable in honing your public speaking skills. Rehearse your speech multiple times, first alone and then in front of a trusted friend or mentor who can provide constructive criticism. Consider recording yourself to identify areas for improvement, such as pacing or clarity. Joining public speaking clubs like Toastmasters can also be incredibly beneficial. These clubs offer a supportive environment where you can practice regularly, receive feedback, and learn from experienced speakers. By embracing these opportunities, you build confidence and refine your skills, making public speaking less daunting and more about sharing your ideas effectively.

Visualization Exercise

- Find a Quiet Space: Sit comfortably and close your eyes.
- Imagine the Room: Picture the venue, the audience, and the stage.
- Visualize Success: See yourself speaking confidently, the audience engaged, and responding positively.
- Breathe Deeply: Inhale slowly through your nose, hold briefly, then exhale through your mouth.
- Repeat: Practice this visualization before each speaking engagement.

This exercise can become part of your preparation routine, helping to calm nerves and instill confidence. Public speaking is not just about relaying information—it's about connecting with your audience and leaving a lasting impression. With practice, the techniques discussed here can help transform public speaking from a source of anxiety into an opportunity for growth and influence.

2.4 Networking 101:

Building Authentic Professional Relationships

Networking often conjures images of awkward small talk at industry mixers, but its true essence goes far beyond that. At its core, networking is about creating meaningful connections that can propel your career forward. It's the bridge between where you are and where you want to be professionally. In today's competitive job market, having a solid network can open doors to opportunities and resources that might otherwise remain out of reach. Imagine you're an artist seeking gallery representation. A well-connected network could connect you with gallery owners, fellow artists, and collectors who appreciate your work, thus expanding your visibility and potential market.

To network effectively, begin with a strong elevator pitch. This concise statement encapsulates who you are, what you do, and what you aim to achieve. Picture this: you're at a conference and find yourself next to someone influential in your field. A well-crafted pitch allows you to introduce yourself confidently, sparking their interest and setting the stage for further conversation. Keep it brief, about 30 seconds, and tailor it to your audience. Practice until it feels natural, as this will help you convey authenticity. After making initial contact, the follow-up is crucial. Send a thank-you note or connect on LinkedIn with a personalized message. Mention something specific from your conversation to jog their memory and reinforce your interest in staying connected. This follow-up shows initiative and keeps the line of communication open.

Authenticity is the cornerstone of effective networking. People are drawn to genuine interactions where both parties stand to benefit. When you approach networking with sincerity, you build trust and rapport, essential for long-lasting professional relationships. Avoid putting on a facade or promise more than you can deliver. Instead, seek to understand others' needs and offer help where you can. This might be as simple as sharing an article relevant to their work or introducing them to someone in your network who could assist with their goals. By building genuine connections rather than merely collecting contacts, you foster mutually beneficial and sustainable relationships over time.

Consider the story of a young marketing professional I know who landed a dream job through networking. While attending a casual networking event, she struck up a conversation with a company executive. Rather than immediately pitching herself for a job, she asked insightful questions about the industry, showing genuine interest and knowledge. This approach impressed the executive, leading to an exchange of contact information. She followed up with a thank-you email, expressing her eagerness to learn more about the company. Months later, when a position opened, the executive remembered her initiative and reached out. This opportunity came from being in the right place at the right time and building a sincere professional relationship based on mutual respect and interest.

Networking is more than personal advancement; it's about creating a supportive community where everyone can thrive. As you build your network, remember that every interaction has the potential to shape your career path. Approach each connection with openness and authenticity. Whether you're at a formal industry event or chatting with a colleague over coffee, these moments can lead to unexpected opportunities and lasting relationships. Building a robust professional network is an investment in your future, one that pays dividends in opportunities, knowledge, and support throughout your career.

2.5 Social Media Savvy:

Communicating Effectively Online

In today's digital age, social media is the megaphone of your personal and professional life. Understanding how to navigate this landscape is crucial for maintaining a positive presence. Each platform has its own vibe, requiring you to tailor your content accordingly. On Instagram, visuals reign supreme, so focus on eye-catching photos and videos. LinkedIn, however, demands a more professional tone, where sharing industry insights or career milestones can showcase your expertise. Twitter thrives on brevity and wit, allowing you to engage in real-time conversations on trending topics. Adjusting your messaging to fit each audience ensures your voice resonates and reaches the right people.

Your online persona is an extension of yourself, and maintaining a consistent image across platforms is vital. This consistency builds trust and authenticity, making your digital footprint more impactful. Imagine a friend who presents a professional demeanor on LinkedIn but shares reckless content on other platforms. Such inconsistencies can confuse or alienate potential employers or collaborators. Your digital footprint is like a public resume, so curate it thoughtfully. Keep your messaging aligned with your personal and professional values. This alignment reinforces your identity and enhances how others perceive you, ultimately opening doors to opportunities.

Engaging with others on social media requires finesse. Responding to comments and messages is an art, balancing authenticity and diplomacy. When handling negative feedback, approach it constructively. Acknowledge the person's concerns and offer a thoughtful response. This not only diffuses tension but also demonstrates maturity and professionalism. For example, suppose a customer complains about a product issue. In that case, responding with empathy and a willingness to resolve the matter can turn a negative interaction into a positive one. Engaging authentically with your audience fosters community and builds relationships. Whether it's a simple "thank you" for a compliment or a more in-depth conversation, these interactions create a sense of connection.

Using social media responsibly involves understanding its ethical dimensions, and respecting privacy and intellectual property is paramount. Always obtain consent before sharing someone else's content, credit the original creator, and be mindful of what you post or share about others. Protecting your and others' privacy online is crucial in maintaining a respectful and safe digital environment. Furthermore, consider the implications of your words and actions. Social media is a powerful tool that can amplify voices for better or worse. Use it to uplift, inform, and inspire rather than to spread negativity or misinformation. By adopting a responsible approach, you contribute to a healthier online community.

The influence of social media on communication cannot be overstated. It provides a platform for expression, connection, and learning. By mastering the nuances of each platform, maintaining a consistent persona, engaging meaningfully, and upholding ethical standards, you can navigate the digital world with confidence and integrity. These skills will enhance your online presence and enrich your personal and professional interactions. As we move forward, remember that your digital identity is as significant as your real-world one. Embrace the power of social media wisely, and let it be a tool for growth and opportunity.

Chapter 3

Navigating the Workplace:

Career Development and Success

Imagine this: You've just graduated, degree in hand, and the world feels wide open. Excitement buzzes in the air as you contemplate your first real job. But then reality hits—how do you even start the job hunt? The first step in this journey is creating a resume and cover letter that stands out in a sea of applicants. These documents are your professional handshake and the first impression you make of potential employers. Think of them as your personal billboard, showcasing who you are and what you can bring to the table. They must be crafted with care and precision, which can mean the difference between landing an interview or getting passed over.

Your resume is a snapshot of your professional life, highlighting your skills, experiences, and accomplishments. There are different types of resumes that you can use depending on your circumstances. The chronological resume lists your work experiences in reverse order, focusing on your career progression. This format is ideal if you have a steady work history in a particular field. On the other hand, a functional resume emphasizes skills and abilities rather than chronological work history, which can be beneficial if you're changing careers or have gaps in employment. The correct format is crucial in presenting your strengths in the best light possible.

Tailoring your resume and cover letter to each job application is crucial. Start by carefully reading the job description and identifying key phrases and requirements. Incorporate these keywords into your resume to demonstrate that you meet the employer's needs. For instance, if a job listing emphasizes teamwork and problem-solving, ensure these skills are prominently featured in your documents. Highlight relevant experiences and accomplishments that align with the job's demands. A cover letter should complement your resume by expanding on your qualifications and conveying your enthusiasm for the role. Personalize it by addressing it to the hiring manager and referencing specific aspects of the company that resonate with you.

Formatting your resume and cover letter for clarity and professionalism enhances readability and impact. Use a consistent font and spacing throughout, such as Arial or Times New Roman, in sizes that are easy to read. Stick to one-inch margins and organize content with clear headings and bullet points. This layout ensures that information is accessible and easy to scan, which is essential since hiring managers often have limited time to review each application. Avoid clutter and keep your content concise, focusing on the most relevant details. Proofread meticulously to eliminate errors that could undermine your credibility.

3.1 Sample Resume and Cover Letter

Consider a young professional applying for a marketing role. Her resume highlights her internship at a digital marketing agency, where she led a successful social media campaign that increased engagement by 30%. She lists content creation and analytics skills aligning with the job's requirements. Her cover letter begins with an engaging introduction: "As a recent graduate with a passion for digital marketing, I am thrilled to apply for the Marketing Coordinator position at XYZ Company." She then shares a specific achievement, "During my internship at ABC Agency, I developed a social media strategy that boosted client engagement by 30%." Her letter concludes with a strong call to action: "I am eager to bring my skills and enthusiasm to XYZ Company and contribute to your team's success." This example demonstrates how personalization and specificity can make your application stand out.

Creating a standout resume and cover letter requires attention to detail, strategic customization, and a clear understanding of what employers seek. These documents serve as your introduction to potential employers, highlighting your strengths and setting the stage for further engagement. With a well-crafted resume and cover letter, you can confidently enter the job market, ready to seize opportunities.

3.2 Acing the Job Interview:

Practical Tips and Tricks

Imagine standing outside the interview room, heart pounding, palms slightly sweaty. The anticipation of making a lasting impression is both exhilarating and nerve-wracking. Preparing for this pivotal moment involves a series of deliberate steps that set you up for success. Start with thorough research of the company you're interviewing with. Understanding their culture and values provides a contextual backdrop for your responses. It's like knowing the rules of a game before playing. If a company prides itself on innovation, highlight your creative problem-solving skills. Dive into their website, read recent news articles, and even check out employee reviews to glean insights into their work environment. This knowledge boosts your confidence and demonstrates genuine interest, which is a quality employers always appreciate.

Next, prepare answers to common interview questions. You'll likely encounter classics like "Tell me about yourself" or "What are your strengths and weaknesses?" Crafting responses that are both authentic and aligned with the job's requirements is vital. Practice articulating your thoughts clearly and concisely, allowing your personality to shine through. Reflect on experiences that demonstrate your skills and adaptability. Structure your answers using the STAR method—Situation, Task, Action, Result. This framework helps you convey experiences in a way that showcases your contributions and outcomes. For example, if asked about a challenging project, describe the context, the role you played, the actions you took, and the positive result.

Interview anxiety is natural but manageable with the proper techniques. Mindfulness exercises can be your secret weapon. Before walking into the interview, take a moment to focus on your breathing. Inhale deeply, hold for a few seconds, then exhale slowly. This simple practice calms nerves and centers your mind. Visualize a positive outcome—seeing yourself confidently answering questions and connecting with the interviewer. This mental rehearsal eases tension and boosts self-assurance. Remember, a little nervousness is natural and can actually enhance your performance by keeping you alert and engaged.

Body language is crucial in shaping the interviewer's perception of you. Maintain eye contact to convey confidence and interest. It's a silent affirmation of your engagement in the conversation. A confident posture, with shoulders back and head held high, signals self-assuredness. Avoid crossing your arms, which can seem defensive, and instead, use open gestures to foster a sense of connection. Smiling genuinely at appropriate moments can also humanize the interaction, creating a friendly atmosphere. These non-verbal cues complement your verbal responses, painting a complete picture of professionalism and approachability.

Once the interview concludes, the process isn't over. Following up is critical to reinforce your interest and leave a lasting impression. Within 24 hours, send a thank-you email to express gratitude for the opportunity. Reference specific points from the interview to personalize your message. For example, "I appreciated the discussion about the company's upcoming projects and am excited about the potential to contribute." This thoughtful gesture shows professionalism and reinforces your enthusiasm for the role.

Additionally, reflect on the interview experience. Consider what went well and identify areas for improvement. This self-assessment is invaluable for future interviews, helping you refine your approach and build on your strengths.

Navigating the interview process involves a blend of preparation, self-awareness, and adaptability. By researching the company, practicing responses, managing anxiety, and mastering body language, you set the stage for a successful interview. Following up with a thoughtful thank-you email and reflecting on your performance completes the cycle, ensuring you continuously grow and improve. Each interview is a learning opportunity, bringing you closer to the role that aligns with your aspirations and skills.

3.3 Building Your Personal Brand:

LinkedIn and Beyond

Personal branding is a concept that might sound like it's reserved for influencers or CEOs. Still, it applies to anyone looking to make their mark professionally. Think of your personal brand as the unique impression you leave behind, encompassing your skills, values, and personality. It's the story of who you are and what you stand for, told through how you present yourself online and offline.

A strong personal brand opens doors by making you memorable to potential employers, collaborators, and clients. It sets you apart in a crowded job market, ensuring that when opportunities arise, you're the one who comes to mind.

Your professional image should be consistent across all platforms, creating a unified narrative about who you are. LinkedIn is a powerful tool in this respect, offering a space to showcase your professional achievements and connect with others in your industry. Start by crafting a compelling headline and summary. Your headline should succinctly capture your career aspirations and current role, like "Aspiring Marketing Specialist with a Passion for Digital Storytelling." This immediately tells visitors what you're about. Your summary, or the "About" section, is where you delve deeper, sharing your professional journey, key accomplishments, and what drives you. Keep it concise but engaging, using a conversational tone to make it relatable.

Showcasing your achievements and endorsements is another way to enhance your LinkedIn profile. Use the "Experience" section to highlight your roles, focusing on what you accomplished rather than just listing responsibilities. Instead of "Managed a team of interns," say, "Led a team of five interns to successfully complete a market analysis project, increasing departmental efficiency by 20%." Quantifying your achievements provides concrete evidence of your impact. Don't hesitate to request endorsements from colleagues or supervisors who can vouch for your skills. These endorsements add credibility and demonstrate that others recognize your expertise.

Networking is integral to personal branding, and LinkedIn is built for this purpose. Join industry-specific groups and participate in discussions to connect with like-minded professionals. Sharing relevant content, such as articles, insights, or even your own blog posts, showcases your expertise and keeps you visible in your network. Engaging with content shared by others can also spark conversations and lead to meaningful connections. Remember, networking is not just about what you can gain but also what you can offer. Providing value to your connections through advice, resources, or introductions strengthens your relationships and enhances your brand.

One example of successful personal branding can be seen in the profile of an industry leader I know who transformed her career through strategic branding on LinkedIn. She started by revamping her profile, focusing on her achievements in healthcare innovation. Her headline read, "Healthcare Innovator | Transforming Patient Care with Technology." Her summary told her career path story, emphasizing milestones aligned with her goals. She regularly shared articles on healthcare trends and participated in discussions, gradually building a reputation as a thought leader. Her efforts paid off when she was approached by a top company for a leadership position, a testament to the power of a well-crafted personal brand.

Building your personal brand is an ongoing process that requires authenticity and consistency. It's about telling your story in a way that resonates with others and aligns with your career goals. By optimizing your LinkedIn profile, showcasing achievements, and actively networking, you create a strong foundation for your brand. This foundation supports your current aspirations and adapts as you grow and evolve in your career, ensuring that you remain relevant and impactful in your field.

3.4 Navigating Workplace Dynamics and Politics

Stepping into the workplace can feel like entering a new ecosystem, teeming with its own set of dynamics and intricacies. Understanding these dynamics is crucial for thriving in any job environment. Within this ecosystem, interpersonal relationships and power structures are always at play. You will encounter key stakeholders and influencers—those individuals who hold sway over decisions and can impact your career progression. Identifying these people early on is vital. Pay attention to who leads meetings, whose opinions are valued, and who your colleagues turn to for advice. These individuals hold unofficial power, and aligning yourself with them can provide invaluable support and guidance. Navigating workplace politics demands a strategic approach. Building alliances with colleagues is one effective way to manage complex office environments. Forming genuine relationships with your peers can create a support network that offers assistance during challenging times. It's not about forming cliques or engaging in favoritism but cultivating mutual respect and collaboration. Additionally, maintaining professionalism in difficult situations is essential. There will be times when emotions run high, or you face adversity, but responding with composure and integrity sets you apart. Remember to focus on facts and solutions rather than personal attacks. This approach resolves conflicts more efficiently and enhances your reputation as a reliable team player.

Emotional intelligence is a cornerstone of successful workplace interactions. It involves recognizing and managing your own emotions while being attuned to the feelings of others. This self-awareness allows you to navigate relationships more effectively, fostering a positive work environment. For instance, when receiving positive or negative feedback, respond constructively. Acknowledge the feedback, thank the person for their input, and consider how you can use it for personal growth. This response demonstrates maturity and a willingness to improve, which are highly valued qualities in any professional setting. By cultivating empathy and understanding, you enhance your ability to connect with colleagues, leading to more harmonious and productive collaborations.

Consider a scenario where you find yourself in disagreement with a supervisor. Perhaps a project deadline was missed, and tensions are high. Instead of approaching the situation defensively, take a step back and assess the circumstances. Initiate a conversation with your supervisor, expressing your understanding of the project's importance and your commitment to resolving the issue. For example, you might say, "I understand the project's impact on our team's goals, and I want to ensure we meet expectations moving forward. How can I improve my performance as a member of this team?" This approach shifts the focus from blame to collaboration, opening the door for constructive dialogue and compromise. Your supervisor will likely appreciate your proactive attitude and willingness to find a solution, ultimately strengthening your working relationship.

Navigating workplace dynamics and politics is a nuanced endeavor that requires a blend of strategic thinking, emotional intelligence, and interpersonal skills. You position yourself as a valuable team member by identifying key stakeholders, building relationships, and maintaining professionalism. Understanding and managing emotions, yours and others, is pivotal in fostering a positive work environment. Whether handling disagreements or receiving feedback, your approach can significantly impact your career trajectory. As you engage with your colleagues and navigate the complexities of workplace politics, remember that every interaction is an opportunity to build trust, demonstrate your capabilities, and contribute meaningfully to your team.

3.5 Continuous Learning:

Upskilling for Career Growth

In today's fast-paced job market, where technology and industries evolve at lightning speed, continuous learning isn't just a nice-to-have; it's a necessity. Upskilling is the answer to staying relevant and competitive in your field. Imagine the workplace as a constantly shifting landscape where new tools, technologies, and methodologies emerge regularly. To thrive, you must be adaptable and ready to embrace these changes. By keeping your skills up-to-date, you enhance your value to your current employer and open doors to new opportunities that align with the latest industry trends.

Identifying which skills to develop can be a daunting task, but it starts with self-assessment. Reflect on your current skills and compare them to the demands of your industry. Are there areas where you feel less confident, or your knowledge might be outdated? Use self-assessment tools like online quizzes or skill inventories to pinpoint these gaps. Feedback from peers and mentors can also provide valuable insights. They might see strengths or weaknesses you hadn't considered. By understanding where you stand, you can create a targeted plan for growth that focuses on areas most likely to benefit your career.

Once you identify the skills you need, explore the myriad of learning opportunities available. Online courses and certifications are a fantastic way to gain new knowledge. Platforms like Coursera, Udemy, and LinkedIn Learning offer courses on everything from coding to project management, many culminating in certifications recognized by employers. These flexible courses can be tailored to fit your schedule, allowing you to learn at your own pace. Additionally, professional workshops and seminars provide hands-on learning experiences and networking opportunities. Attending industry conferences can also be a valuable way to stay informed about the latest developments and connect with other professionals.

Consider the story of a colleague who pivoted her career by embracing continuous learning. After years in a traditional marketing role, she realized the digital landscape was transforming her field. She enrolled in a series of online courses focused on digital marketing strategies and tools. Over time, she earned certifications in SEO and social media management. This dedication to upskilling opened the door to a position as a digital marketing manager at a leading tech company. Her commitment to learning enhanced her professional skills and reignited her passion for her work.

Continuous learning is more than just keeping up with the times; it's about taking charge of your career trajectory. By staying informed and adaptable, you position yourself as a valuable asset in any workplace. The skills you acquire today could be the ones that set you apart tomorrow, making you the go-to person for innovative solutions and fresh ideas. In an ever-changing world, the commitment to learning keeps you moving forward, ready to tackle new challenges and seize exciting opportunities.

3.6 Understanding Employment Benefits:

Making the Most of Your Package

Starting a new job is more than just an opportunity to earn a paycheck; it's also about understanding and leveraging the benefits that come with it. Employment benefits are essential to your compensation package, often providing more value than you might initially realize. Health insurance is one of employers' most common and critical benefits. It helps cover medical expenses and can significantly reduce the financial burden of healthcare. Within health insurance, you'll find various plans, such as Health Maintenance Organizations (HMO), Preferred Provider Organizations (PPO), and High Deductible Health Plans (HDHP). Each type has pros and cons; understanding these will help you choose the best option for your needs.

Additionally, retirement plans like 401(k)s are crucial for building a secure financial future. Many employers offer matching contributions, essentially free money that boosts your retirement savings. Taking full advantage of these contributions can significantly impact your long-term economic health.

When evaluating and selecting benefits, it's essential to approach the task with a strategic mindset. Start by comparing health plan options carefully. Consider factors like premium costs, deductibles, and the network of doctors and hospitals. If you have specific healthcare needs, ensure that your chosen plan covers them adequately. Understanding employer contributions is another crucial aspect. Some employers may cover a large portion of the premium costs, making specific plans more affordable. Evaluate how these contributions affect your out-of-pocket expenses to make an informed decision. It's not just about selecting the cheapest option but finding the balance between cost and coverage that works best for you.

Beyond the standard benefits, there are often lesser-known options that can provide immense value. Employee assistance programs (EAPs) are a great example. These programs offer services like counseling, mental health support, and financial advice, often at no cost to you. They can be a lifeline during stressful times, providing resources to help you manage personal or work-related challenges. Professional development funds are another underutilized benefit. Some employers allocate money for employees to attend workshops, conferences, or courses that enhance their skills. Taking advantage of these opportunities boosts your career and demonstrates your commitment to growth and learning.

To maximize your benefits, it's essential to be proactive. Regularly review and update your benefit selections, especially during open enrollment periods. As your life circumstances change, so might your needs. For instance, if you get married or have a child, you might need to adjust your health coverage. Staying informed about any changes your employer makes to the benefits package ensures you remain aligned with your goals.

Additionally, utilize wellness programs offered by your employer. These programs often include gym memberships, health screenings, or wellness challenges promoting healthier lifestyles.

Participating in these can improve your well-being and even lead to savings through reduced health premiums or incentives.

Understanding and leveraging employment benefits is an integral part of your professional life. It's not just about the immediate perks but about building a foundation for a stable and fulfilling future. As you navigate your career, these benefits can provide security, enhance your skills, and support your well-being. By making informed choices and actively engaging with your benefits, you maximize their value, setting yourself up for success in the present and future.

Chapter 4

Time Management

And a Healthy Work-Life Balance

Picture this: You wake up to the blaring sound of your alarm, a to-do list spiraling through your head before your feet even hit the floor. The day stretches ahead, a tangled web of tasks and obligations. Welcome to the modern juggling act of work-life balance. For young adults, managing time effectively is not just a skill; it's a lifeline. It's about finding harmony in the chaos, ensuring that both professional ambitions and personal passions thrive. This chapter will guide you through the art of prioritizing tasks to transform your busy life into a symphony of productivity and satisfaction.

Prioritizing tasks is more than just checking items off a list. It's about understanding what truly matters and making informed decisions about how you spend your time. Differentiating between urgent and important tasks is vital. Urgent tasks scream for immediate attention, like replying to a time-sensitive email or meeting a fast-approaching deadline. They're the squeaky wheels of your day. Essential tasks, however, contribute to your long-term goals and values. They might not demand immediate action but are crucial for personal growth and success. Understanding this distinction helps you allocate time wisely, ensuring that urgency doesn't overshadow significance.

One effective method for prioritizing tasks is the Eisenhower Box, a tool named after Dwight Eisenhower, the 34th President of the United States. This method categorizes tasks into four sections: urgent and important, important but not urgent, urgent but not important, and neither urgent nor important. Tasks that are both urgent and important are top priorities and should be tackled immediately. Important but not urgent tasks, like planning a future project, should be scheduled for later. Urgent but not important tasks can often be delegated, freeing your time for more significant endeavors. Finally, tasks that are neither urgent nor important should be eliminated, as they add little value to your day. By consistently applying these categories, you focus on what truly matters, enhancing productivity and satisfaction (SOURCE 1).

The ABCD prioritization system offers another practical approach. Here, you categorize tasks by importance with letters: A for the most critical tasks, B for tasks you should do, C for tasks that are nice to do, and D for tasks that can be delegated or postponed. Begin each day by reviewing your list and assigning letters based on their impact and urgency. This system provides clarity and structure, guiding you through the inevitable chaos of a busy schedule.

Yet, even with the best-laid plans, unexpected tasks can arise, threatening to derail your day. Flexibility is key. Build buffer times into your schedule instead of letting these surprises throw you off balance. This proactive approach allows you to accommodate unforeseen demands without compromising your priorities. Procrastination is another common challenge, often exacerbated by the overwhelming nature of a long to-do list. Combat this by breaking tasks into smaller, manageable steps. This makes them less intimidating and more achievable, encouraging steady progress rather than paralysis.

In our digital age, task management tools can be invaluable allies. To-do list apps like Todoist offer reminders and project organization features, helping you track tasks and deadlines. These apps sync across devices, ensuring you stay on top of your responsibilities at home or on the go. Calendar blocking is another powerful technique. Allocate specific time slots for different activities, creating a visual representation of your day. This helps you allocate time effectively and provides a clear overview of your commitments, reducing the likelihood of overbooking or double scheduling.

Interactive Element: Task Prioritization Exercise

- List Your Tasks: Write down all the tasks you must complete this week.
- Use the Eisenhower Box: Categorize each task into the four quadrants.
- Apply the ABCD System: Assign letters to tasks based on importance.
- Reflect: Consider how these tools change your approach to your workload.

Experiment with these techniques and tools to find what resonates with your lifestyle. Mastering task prioritization transforms chaos into clarity, paving the way for a balanced and happy life.

4.1 Setting Boundaries:

Protecting Your Personal Time

In the rush of modern life, setting boundaries becomes a lifeline for preserving your personal time and sanity. Boundaries are not just about saying no; they are about safeguarding the spaces where you recharge and relax. When you establish clear work hours and personal time, you carve out moments that belong solely to you, reducing stress and preventing burnout. Think of boundaries as invisible fences that keep work from encroaching on your evenings or weekends. They allow you to enjoy hobbies, spend time with loved ones, and simply unwind. Without these boundaries, work-life balance becomes a distant dream, leaving you feeling like you're always on call, never genuinely off-duty.

Communication is crucial in asserting and maintaining these boundaries. Using "I" statements can help you express your needs without sounding accusatory. For example, instead of saying, "You're always emailing me after hours," try, "I feel overwhelmed when I receive work emails at night. Can we agree to limit communication to work hours?" This approach clarifies your feelings and opens the door to constructive dialogue. It's about making your needs known while respecting others' perspectives. Handling boundary violations diplomatically is equally important. When someone crosses a line, address it calmly and directly. You might say, "I understand this is important, but I must stick to my work hours. Let's schedule a time to discuss this during the day." You reinforce your boundaries without damaging relationships by handling such situations with poise.

Setting boundaries isn't always easy. You might face guilt or pushback, especially if others aren't used to you asserting your limits. It's natural to feel guilty for prioritizing your personal time, but remember that setting boundaries is an act of self-care, not selfishness. It's about ensuring you have the energy to give your best at work and in life. Pushback can come from colleagues or even yourself, as old habits die hard. However, standing firm and reminding yourself of the benefits can help you stay resolute. It's a gradual process, but it becomes easier to uphold your boundaries and enjoy the balance they bring with practice.

Consider the story of a remote worker who learned the value of boundaries while balancing work and family. Initially, she struggled with constant work interruptions, as work emails and calls bled into her family time. She set clear work hours, communicating them to her team and family. "From 9 to 5, I'm fully available," she told her colleagues. "After that, I'm offline with family." Implementing this boundary allowed her to focus on her tasks without distraction and be present with her family in the evenings. The transition wasn't without its bumps, but by staying firm and consistent, she found a rhythm that worked. Her productivity improved, and her family appreciated her undivided attention. This story illustrates how setting and maintaining boundaries can create a harmonious balance between work and personal life.

Establishing boundaries is more than managing time; it's about asserting your right to a fulfilling life outside of work. The clarity and peace that come from well-defined boundaries are invaluable, offering you the space to breathe, reflect, and engage meaningfully with the world around you. Embracing this practice enhances your work-life balance and enriches your overall well-being.

4.2 Creating a Flexible Schedule That Works for You

Have you ever noticed how some days start with a burst of energy while others feel sluggish from the get-go? This ebb and flow of energy is a natural part of life, and a flexible schedule can help you harness these fluctuations to boost productivity and well-being. Unlike rigid routines that demand adherence to a strict timetable, a flexible schedule adapts to your unique rhythms, allowing you to work when you're most productive and take breaks when needed. This approach enhances satisfaction in both work and personal life, creating a balance that feels less like a juggling act and more like a well-choreographed dance.

To design a schedule that fits your life, start by identifying your peak productivity times. Are you an early bird who thrives in the morning, or do you find your groove in the afternoon? Use this self-awareness to structure your day around these peak periods. During these times, tackle your most demanding tasks, reserving less critical work for when your energy wanes. It's equally important to incorporate breaks and downtime into your schedule. Short breaks can recharge your mind, preventing burnout and maintaining focus. Consider using the Pomodoro Technique, which involves working for 25 minutes followed by a 5-minute break. This method promotes sustained concentration while allowing the brain to rest.

Daily energy fluctuations are inevitable, and your schedule should reflect this reality. Adjustments might include starting work later on days when mornings feel sluggish or scheduling creative tasks for times when you're naturally more inspired. Flexibility is about listening to your body's cues and respecting its needs. This adaptability fosters a sense of autonomy, making work feel less like an obligation and more like a choice. Remember, a flexible schedule is a living document; it evolves as your needs and circumstances change, so regularly reassess and tweak it to maintain effectiveness.

However, maintaining a flexible schedule isn't without its challenges. Distractions can easily creep in, threatening to derail your carefully crafted plans. To combat this, create a dedicated workspace that minimizes interruptions. Inform those around you of your work times, and use tools like noise-canceling headphones to block out background noise. Another challenge is ensuring accountability, especially when working independently. Without the structure of a traditional 9-to-5, it's easy to let tasks slip through the cracks. Establishing clear goals and deadlines can provide the structure needed to stay on track. Additionally, consider using scheduling apps like Google Calendar or Doodle to plan your day and set reminders for important tasks.

Let's look at someone who has successfully implemented a flexible schedule. Take Jamie, a freelancer juggling multiple projects. Initially overwhelmed by the sheer volume of work, Jamie realized that a rigid 9-to-5 approach wasn't cutting it. Instead, he embraced a flexible schedule, mapping out his days around peak productivity times. Mornings became dedicated to writing and creative tasks, while afternoons focused on client meetings and emails. Jamie also built in time for yoga and walks, which helped maintain energy levels. By adjusting his schedule to align with natural rhythms, Jamie increased productivity and found greater enjoyment in his work. This approach allowed more time for personal interests, creating a harmonious balance between professional responsibilities and personal passions.

A flexible schedule can be your greatest ally in today's fast-paced world. It allows you to blend work and life in an authentic and fulfilling way. By tailoring your schedule to your unique needs and embracing the fluidity of life, you open the door to greater productivity, satisfaction, and well-being.

4.3 Digital Detox:

Balancing Screen Time and Personal Life

In today's digital age, screens are everywhere. From the moment you wake up to the time you drift off to sleep, your phone, computer, or TV is likely within arm's reach. While technology connects us and offers endless information, excessive screen time can take a toll on both mental and physical health. Constant connectivity can lead to burnout, where the boundary between work and personal life blurs, making it hard to disconnect. Sleep quality often suffers when screens dominate your evenings. The blue light emitted by devices can interfere with your body's natural sleep cycle, making it harder to fall and stay asleep. Additionally, being constantly plugged in increases stress levels, as notifications and alerts keep your mind engaged long after your workday ends. This perpetual state of alertness can leave you feeling frazzled and overwhelmed, impacting your personal and professional life.

Reducing screen time is crucial for maintaining balance and reclaiming your well-being. One effective strategy is implementing tech-free zones in your home. Designate specific areas, like the dining room or bedroom, where screens are off-limits. This encourages face-to-face interactions with family or roommates and fosters a more relaxed environment. Setting screen time limits on your devices can also help you disconnect. Utilize built-in features on smartphones or apps that track your usage and remind you when it's time to unplug. Establishing specific times each day when you put your devices away can create a healthier relationship with technology. These limits remind you to engage with the world around you, offering a chance to recharge mentally and physically.

The benefits of a digital detox are profound. By reducing screen time, you'll likely notice improved focus and productivity. Without constant distractions, your mind can concentrate more fully on tasks, enhancing efficiency. In personal interactions, being fully present allows for deeper connections and more meaningful conversations. You might find yourself listening intently and engaging more thoughtfully with those around you. This enhanced presence can strengthen relationships, creating greater fulfillment and satisfaction.

Consider the concept of a weekend digital detox challenge. Picture this: you commit to spending one weekend unplugged from all screens a month. Instead of scrolling through social media, you explore local parks, pick up a new hobby, or simply enjoy the company of friends and family. One friend of mine embraced this practice, setting aside one weekend each month to disconnect completely. At first, it felt strange and uncomfortable, but the benefits became apparent over time. She was more relaxed and refreshed, with a newfound appreciation for the world beyond her screens. This monthly ritual soon became a cherished part of her routine, offering her a much-needed respite from the constant buzz of technology.

Embracing a digital detox doesn't mean abandoning technology altogether. It's about finding a balance that allows you to enjoy connectivity's benefits without being overwhelmed. Taking deliberate steps to reduce screen time opens the door to a more mindful and fulfilling life. This balance is essential in a world where screens are omnipresent, and disconnecting becomes valuable in maintaining your well-being.

4.4 Self-Care Routines for a Balanced Life

Picture this: you're feeling overwhelmed by work demands, your social life is hectic, and your personal time seems to have vanished. It's easy to overlook the quiet power of self-care in maintaining balance amidst life's whirlwind. Self-care is more than just pampering yourself; it's a holistic approach encompassing physical, mental, and emotional well-being. It's about nurturing yourself so you can thrive, not just survive. When you prioritize self-care, you create a foundation of resilience that supports you through stressful and challenging situations. This will give you the confidence to help and support others in crisis.

Incorporating self-care into your daily routine doesn't have to be an elaborate affair. Start with simple practices that fit seamlessly into your life.

A morning routine might include:

- Stretching.
- A few minutes of meditation.
- Savoring a quiet cup of coffee before diving into your day.

An evening routine could involve:

- Preparing a healthy dinner.
- Winding down with a good book.
- Take a warm bath to signal your body that it's time to rest.

These small rituals act as anchors, grounding you amidst the chaos. Scheduling regular leisure activities, like a weekly yoga class or a weekend hike, ensures you carve out time for enjoyment and relaxation. These moments recharge your spirit, making you more resilient to the demands of daily life.

However, self-care often faces barriers, with time constraints being a common culprit. When your schedule is packed, finding time for self-care might seem impossible. Yet, integrating these practices into your day doesn't require hours of free time. It's about making intentional choices. For instance, combine exercise with your commute by biking to work or taking the stairs instead of the elevator. These small changes add up, infusing your day with moments of self-care. Another hurdle is overcoming the guilt associated with taking time for yourself. Society often glorifies busyness, equating rest with laziness. Reframing this mindset is crucial, recognizing that self-care is a necessity, not a luxury. Caring for yourself makes you better equipped to meet responsibilities and support those around you.

Let's look at some examples of effective self-care routines. Consider Alex, who juggles a demanding job with many social commitments. To maintain balance, Alex dedicates ten minutes each morning to mindfulness meditation. This practice centers

Alex, providing a calm start to the day. In the evenings, Alex unwinds by cooking a healthy meal, turning a routine task into a moment of creativity and nourishment. It's important to start and end your days with calm confidence.

Similarly, Max, a college student, incorporates regular exercise into his week. By joining a local running group, Max combines physical activity with social interaction, nurturing both body and mind. These routines highlight how self-care can be personalized and woven into everyday life, enhancing overall well-being and productivity.

Self-care is an ongoing commitment to yourself, a promise to prioritize your needs and well-being amidst the hustle and bustle of life. It's about listening to your body and mind and responding to their cues with kindness and attention. Whether it's a few minutes of solitude or a leisurely afternoon spent doing something you love, self-care is the key to sustaining balance and joy in your life.

4.5 Mindfulness Practices for Stress Reduction

Imagine sitting in a traffic jam, your mind racing with a thousand thoughts about the day ahead. Stress levels soar as you juggle responsibilities at work and home. In such moments, mindfulness offers a refuge—a tool for managing stress and enhancing well-being. Mindfulness is the practice of anchoring your attention to the present moment and observing your thoughts and feelings without judgment. This simple act can significantly reduce stress by breaking the cycle of worry about the past or future. By cultivating present-moment awareness, you create a space where calmness can flourish, helping you respond to life's challenges with clarity rather than reactivity.

Incorporating mindfulness into daily life doesn't require hours of meditation or dramatic lifestyle changes. Start with something as simple as a breathing exercise. Find a quiet space, close your eyes, and focus on your breath. Inhale deeply through your nose, hold for a moment, then exhale slowly through your mouth. Notice the sensation of air moving in and out of your body. This exercise anchors you in the present, drawing your focus away from stressors. For a more dynamic approach, try mindful walking. As you walk, pay attention to each step, the sensation of your feet touching the ground, and the rhythm of your movement. Or, embrace mindful eating by savoring each bite and noticing the flavors and textures. These practices transform ordinary activities into opportunities for mindfulness, seamlessly integrating into your routine.

Maintaining a consistent mindfulness practice poses challenges. The busyness of life can make finding time for mindfulness seem elusive. However, remember that mindfulness doesn't demand large chunks of time. Even a few minutes daily can make a difference. Set aside a specific time each day, perhaps during your morning coffee or before bed, to practice mindfulness. Consistency, not duration, is vital. Another challenge is maintaining focus and discipline. Your mind will wander—it's natural. When it does, gently guide your attention back to the present moment without judgment. Returning to the present is an exercise in mindfulness, strengthening your ability to focus over time.

Consider the experience of a professional who turned to mindfulness to manage workplace stress. Each day, she found herself overwhelmed by endless emails and tight deadlines. Stress began affecting her health and relationships. Committed to change, she introduced a mindfulness routine into her mornings. Before diving into work, she spent ten minutes meditating, focusing on her breath, and setting intentions for the day. Gradually, she noticed a shift. Stressors became more manageable, and her ability to focus improved. Mindfulness became her anchor, providing clarity and calm amid the chaos of her demanding job. This practice enhanced her professional life and well-being, illustrating mindfulness's transformative power.

Incorporating mindfulness into your life is a commitment to yourself. It's about carving out moments of peace amidst the noise, reclaiming your calm, and building resilience against stress. These practices nurture your mind and overall well-being, enhancing your capacity to navigate life's challenges with grace and intention. As we move forward, remember that the stress reduction and balance tools are within your reach, ready to be embraced and integrated into your daily life.

PLEASE HELP ME & GEN-Z

Please help another friend or young adult find this helpful guide book by leaving an **Amazon Review**.

Just scroll down to the bottom of this books Amazon page and you will find the **'Write a Review'** button.

It only takes a minute and it will 'make my day'.

You can also leave a photo or short video along with your review. Thank you for your support! Sam Matthews

SCAN ME & LEAVE A REVIEW

Chapter 5

Mastering the Basics:

Cooking, Nutrition, and Home Skills

Picture this: you've just moved into your own place, and the glow of independence is still fresh and exciting. But as dinnertime rolls around, you're staring at your empty kitchen, unsure where to start. You might be tempted to reach for your phone and order takeout, but this is the perfect opportunity to delve into the world of cooking. The kitchen is more than just a place to prepare food; it's a space where creativity meets sustenance, and mastering a few basic skills can transform you from a takeout regular to a confident home cook. Let's demystify some of these foundational techniques that will set you on a culinary journey, starting with boiling, sautéing, and roasting.

Boiling is the simplest of cooking methods, involving immersing food in water or broth and heating it until it bubbles vigorously. It's perfect for pasta, rice, and vegetables. With a pinch of salt, boiling enhances flavors and cooks food evenly. Sautéing, on the other hand, adds flair to your dishes by cooking food quickly in a small amount of oil or butter over medium-high heat. Think sizzling onions for a stir-fry or garlic-infused oil as a base for sauces. Roasting brings out the natural sweetness in vegetables and meats. By cooking at high temperatures, typically in an oven, you achieve a caramelized, crispy exterior while keeping the inside tender. Mastering these techniques opens a world of culinary possibilities, allowing you to prepare delicious meals easily.

Understanding food safety and hygiene is crucial when cooking.

To prevent contamination:

- Wash your hands thoroughly before handling food, especially raw meat or eggs.
- Clean all your utensils and surfaces regularly, and separate raw ingredients from cooked ones to avoid cross-contamination.
- Keep perishable foods refrigerated and use them before their expiration dates to ensure freshness and safety.

These practices keep your meals safe and instill confidence as you experiment in the kitchen.

Let's dive into some simple recipes that even a novice can master. One-pot pasta dishes are a fantastic starting point. Begin by boiling your favorite pasta in a pot. Once al dente, drain and return to the pot, adding your choice of sauce and protein—like chicken or chickpeas—and a handful of spinach or cherry tomatoes. Stir over low heat until everything is warm and well combined. This method is not only easy but also minimizes cleanup, making it ideal for busy days. A basic vegetable stir-fry is another beginner-friendly option. Start by sautéing garlic and onions in a bit of oil, then add a mix of your favorite vegetables—such as bell peppers and broccoli. Finish with a splash of soy sauce and serve over steamed rice for a quick, nutritious meal.

Meal prep and organization are your allies in the kitchen, saving you time and stress throughout the week. Start by planning your meals and creating a shopping list to ensure you have all the necessary ingredients. Once home, wash and chop vegetables, marinate proteins, and portion grains to streamline the cooking process. Store ingredients in labeled containers, making it easy to grab what you need. This preparation speeds up meal time and reduces the temptation to order takeout when you're short on time.

Cooking is an art; like any art form, it thrives on creativity and experimentation. Don't be afraid to play around with recipes and substitute ingredients based on your taste or dietary preferences. Swap out regular pasta for whole wheat or gluten-free alternatives, or replace chicken with tofu for a plant-based dish. These adaptations cater to specific needs and allow you to explore new flavors and textures. Embrace the freedom to make each recipe your own, and soon, you'll find joy in the culinary process.

Interactive Element: Cooking Confidence Checklist

4. Boiling: Have I salted the water? Is the food cooked evenly?
5. Sautéing: Is the oil hot enough to create a sizzle? Are the ingredients cut uniformly?
6. Roasting: Have I preheated the oven? Is the food arranged in a single layer for even cooking?
7. Food Safety: Have I washed my hands and surfaces? Am I avoiding cross-contamination?
8. Meal Prep: Are my ingredients organized and labeled? Do I have a weekly meal plan ready?
9. Experimentation: Have I considered dietary preferences or new flavors? Am I open to trying different ingredients?

This checklist serves as a guide to boost your confidence as you step into the kitchen, ensuring each cooking session is both enjoyable and successful.

5.1 Meal Planning on a Budget:

Eating Healthy Without Breaking the Bank

Imagine walking into your kitchen and knowing exactly what you will eat for the week. It's not just a dream; it's what meal planning can do for you. This approach saves time and cuts down on unnecessary expenses and food waste. By planning your meals, you can take control of your grocery budget and ensure that every item you buy has a purpose. It's about making thoughtful choices that stretch your dollars while ensuring you eat healthily. Reducing food waste is one of the biggest advantages. When you plan, you buy only what you need, which means less food ends up in the trash. This practice not only helps your wallet but also the planet, as it cuts down on the resources used to produce and dispose of food. Maximizing your grocery budget becomes second nature as you learn to plan meals around sales and what you already have in your pantry.

Creating budget-friendly meal plans might sound challenging but easier than you think. One of the simplest strategies is to buy seasonal produce. Fruits and vegetables that are in season are often cheaper and fresher. For example, you might find great deals on berries and tomatoes in summer. In winter, root vegetables like carrots and potatoes become budget-friendly staples. Another tip is to utilize bulk food sections. Buying grains, beans, and spices in bulk can significantly reduce costs. These items store well, so you can buy just what you need without paying for packaging. A well-stocked pantry of bulk items allows for flexibility in meal planning, letting you whip up a variety of dishes without a last-minute grocery run.

Balancing nutrition and cost is crucial when planning meals on a budget. Choose nutrient-dense foods that give you the most bang for your buck. Whole grains, legumes, and fresh produce should make up the bulk of your diet. These foods are filling and packed with essential nutrients, keeping you satisfied and healthy. Meal swapping and batch cooking are also effective strategies. Swap expensive ingredients for more affordable ones. For instance, use lentils instead of ground beef in a chili recipe. This swap saves money and adds a healthy dose of fiber and protein. Batch cooking involves preparing larger quantities of food at once, which you can then portion out for the week. This technique saves time and ensures you always have a healthy meal ready to go.

Let's look at some sample meal plans that are both budget-friendly and nutritious. A weekly vegetarian meal plan might include dishes like chickpea curry, vegetable stir-fry with tofu, and hearty lentil soup. These meals are not only affordable but also rich in protein and fiber. For a family dinner plan under $50, consider recipes like spaghetti with homemade tomato sauce, a baked potato with various toppings, and a simple vegetable stir-fry. Each meal is designed to be filling and nutritious, ensuring everyone is satisfied without breaking the bank.

Meal planning on a budget doesn't mean sacrificing taste or nutrition. It's about making smart choices that benefit your health and your wallet. You can create delicious and healthy meals without overspending by incorporating strategies like buying seasonal produce, utilizing bulk food sections, and focusing on nutrient-dense foods.

5.2 Understanding Nutrition Labels:

Making Informed Choices

Next time you're grocery shopping, take a moment to flip over a package and examine the nutrition label. It may look like a jumble of numbers and words, but understanding this information is key to making healthier food choices. The label provides a breakdown of serving sizes, which is the first step in informed decision-making. Serving sizes are standardized to help you compare similar foods.

For instance, if a cereal box lists a serving size as one cup, but you typically eat two, you'll need to double the nutritional values to know your actual intake. The servings per container tell you how many servings the package contains, revealing how quickly that box might empty.

Macronutrients—carbohydrates, proteins, and fats—are the building blocks of our diet. They provide energy and are crucial for various bodily functions. Carbs fuel your body, proteins are essential for muscle repair, and fats are vital for brain health. The label breaks these down, showing how much each serving contributes to your daily needs. Pay attention to the type of fat listed. While unsaturated fats are beneficial, trans fats are not. These artificial fats can increase bad cholesterol levels and should be avoided. Sodium levels are also critical. Consuming too much can lead to hypertension, so look for products with lower sodium content.

Added sugars are another red flag on labels. The American Heart Association recommends limiting added sugars to no more than 25 grams per day for women and 36 grams for men. These sugars can sneak into foods you wouldn't expect, like bread or salad dressing. Recognizing them can help you make healthier choices. When comparing products, check the ingredients list for words like corn syrup, fructose, and glucose, which all signal added sugars. Understanding health claims is equally important. Words like "low fat" or "high fiber" can be misleading. A product labeled "low fat" might compensate with added sugars, so always verify claims with the actual nutritional data.

Let's consider an example. You're trying to choose between two cereal brands. Start with the serving size and servings per container. Suppose one cereal lists 200 calories per cup and the other 150 calories per three-quarters cup. In that case, you'll need to adjust for a fair comparison. Check macronutrient content next. One might boast higher fiber, which is excellent for digestion, while the other is lower in sugar. This information allows you to pick the cereal that aligns with your health goals.

Another example is yogurt. One brand might advertise itself as "light," but it contains artificial sweeteners and less protein than regular yogurt. By examining protein content and sugar levels, you can select a yogurt that provides real nutritional benefits.

Interactive Element: Nutrition Label Reading Practice

- Step 1: Find a packaged food item in your pantry.
- Step 2: Identify the serving size and servings per container. How do they compare to your usual portion?
- Step 3: Analyze the macronutrient breakdown. Are the carbs, proteins, and fats within your dietary goals?
- Step 4: Look for added sugars and sodium levels. Are they higher or lower than expected?
- Step 5: Verify any health claims on the packaging with the actual nutritional data. Are they justified?

This exercise will help you become more familiar with reading and interpreting nutrition labels, empowering you to confidently make healthier choices.

5.3 Essential Kitchen Skills: From Boiling to Baking

When you step into the kitchen, think of it as your playground, where the right skills can turn any meal into a masterpiece. One of the most fundamental skills is knife handling. Knowing how to chop, dice, and mince makes cooking more efficient and safer. Start by learning the basic grip: wrap your fingers around the handle with your thumb and index finger, pinching the base of the blade. Practice makes perfect, so start with something simple, like an onion. Chopping is about consistent cuts, dicing involves smaller, uniform pieces, and mincing creates fine bits perfect for garlic or herbs. A sharp knife is your best friend, preventing injuries and ensuring precision. Alongside cutting techniques, knowing how to store your food properly is crucial. Keep perishable items like fruits, vegetables, and meats in the fridge, and label leftovers with dates to track freshness. This prevents waste and keeps your kitchen organized.

Baking is another kitchen art worth exploring. It's more science than instinct, so accuracy is vital. Measuring ingredients correctly can make all the difference. Dry measuring cups are used for flour and sugar, and liquid measuring cups for water and milk. Level off dry ingredients using a straight edge for precision. Baking involves terms like "creaming" and "folding," which are essential to understand. Creaming refers to beating butter and sugar together until light and fluffy, creating air pockets that help your baked goods rise. Folding is the gentle incorporation of beaten egg whites or whipped cream into a batter, preserving the air within for a light texture. These techniques are foundational, and practicing them will boost your baking confidence.

A well-organized kitchen can transform your cooking experience. Start by setting up a functional workspace. Keep your most-used tools—like knives, cutting boards, and measuring cups—within easy reach. Invest in a few essential tools, such as a sturdy chef's knife, a reliable set of measuring spoons, and a heavy-duty stand mixer if you bake often. Store pantry staples like flour, sugar, and spices in clear, labeled containers to easily see when supplies run low. Declutter regularly to maintain a tidy environment, which saves time and reduces stress. An organized kitchen is a productive one, allowing you to focus on cooking rather than searching for misplaced utensils.

Practicing these skills is the best way to become comfortable in your kitchen. Start with simple projects that build your confidence, like baking a loaf of bread. The process of mixing, kneading, and watching dough rise teaches patience and attention to detail. Plus, nothing beats the aroma of freshly baked bread wafting through your home. As you gain confidence, experiment with different types of bread, such as whole grain or sourdough. Another project is organizing your pantry. Take everything out, clean the shelves, and categorize items by use. This exercise helps you know what you have and makes finding ingredients a breeze when you're in the middle of cooking.

Cooking and baking are skills that anyone can develop with a bit of practice and patience. Mastering them boosts your culinary repertoire and turns your kitchen into a space of creativity and enjoyment. As you become more skilled, you'll find that cooking isn't just about feeding yourself—it's about discovering flavors, textures, and techniques that bring joy and satisfaction to your everyday life. Next time you have a wonderful meal at a restaurant or a friend's house, look it up on your laptop or smartphone when you get home. You will find dozens of easy-to-follow recipes with video and audio instructions online to try yourself.

5.4 Basic Home Repairs Everyone Should Know

Imagine this: it's late, and every drip from your faucet echoes through the quiet night. Instead of reaching for your phone to call a plumber, consider rolling up your sleeves and tackling the repair yourself. Fixing a leaky faucet is one of those quintessential home repair skills that, once mastered, can save you time and money. Begin by turning off the water supply beneath the sink. Use a wrench to loosen the nuts and remove the faucet handle. Once exposed, you'll often find the culprit—a worn-out washer or O-ring. Replace it with a new one, available at any hardware store, and reassemble the faucet. Turn the water back on and relish in the silence of a drip-free night. This simple repair fixes an annoyance and boosts your confidence in handling other household issues.

Another common annoyance in any home is a clogged drain. A clogged drain can disrupt your daily routine, whether the sink or shower. Start by removing any visible debris, such as hair or food particles, using a pair of gloves or a small tool. If the clog persists, try a mixture of baking soda and vinegar. Pour half a cup of baking soda down the drain, followed by an equal amount of vinegar. Let it sit for 15 minutes before flushing with hot water. For more challenging clogs, a plunger or plumber's snake might be necessary. These tools can dislodge blockages deeper in the pipes, restoring the flow. Regular maintenance and using a drain guard can prevent future clogs, making this repair less frequent.

Patching a hole in drywall is another skill that can come in handy. Whether from moving furniture or an accidental bump, holes happen. Start by cleaning the area around the hole. For small holes, apply a layer of spackle with a putty knife, smoothing it out to blend with the wall. For larger holes, you'll need a patch kit. Cut a piece of drywall to fit, secure it in place, and cover it with a joint compound. Sand it smooth once dry, and finish with a coat of paint to match the wall. This repair restores the appearance of your wall and strengthens it against future impacts.

Changing a light bulb seems straightforward, but it's a task that goes beyond twisting one bulb out and another in. Different fixtures require different approaches. For recessed lighting or chandeliers, you may need a ladder and a steady hand. Always turn off the power to the fixture before starting to prevent any accidents. If you're replacing a fixture entirely, start by unscrewing the old one and disconnecting the wires. Connect the new fixture's wires to the corresponding ones in the ceiling, secure the fixture in place, and turn the power back on. This skill allows you to brighten up your space without waiting for a professional.

Regular maintenance and upkeep around your home can prevent these minor issues from becoming major problems. Routine checks, like testing smoke detectors, will help ensure your home remains safe. Replace batteries every six months and test the alarms monthly. This small task can be lifesaving, providing early warning in case of fire. Similarly, inspect your home for any signs of wear and tear. Look for cracks in the walls, leaks under sinks, or any unusual noises from appliances. Catching these early can save significant time and expense.

Safety should always be your priority when conducting DIY repairs. Use tools correctly, ensuring you have the right one for the job. A toolbox equipped with essentials like a hammer, screwdriver, pliers, and tape measure can tackle most tasks. Always read instructions and watch online tutorials if you're unsure. Sometimes, the best decision is knowing when to call a professional. If a repair involves gas lines, electrical wiring, or structural elements, it's wise to seek expert help. Your safety and that of your home are worth more than the cost of a professional's expertise.

5.5 Cleaning Hacks:

For a Tidy, Stress-Free Environment

The state of your living space often mirrors your mental state. A tidy home is more than just visually appealing; it has a profound impact on your well-being. Imagine walking into a room free of clutter, where everything has its place. The air feels lighter, and you can breathe easier, quite literally. Cleanliness reduces allergens and bacteria, which can improve your health by minimizing respiratory issues and allergies. Beyond the physical, a clean space fosters a calm mind, allowing you to focus and think clearly. It's like a weight lifts off your shoulders when your surroundings are in order.

Keeping your space clean doesn't have to be a monumental task. With a few practical tips, you can maintain a spotless home with minimal effort. Vinegar and baking soda are powerful allies in natural cleaning. Mix them to tackle tough stains or deodorize surfaces. For example, sprinkle baking soda in your sink, then pour vinegar over it, letting it fizz for a few minutes before scrubbing. This method is not only effective but also eco-friendly. Establishing quick daily cleaning routines can make a huge difference. Dedicate just 15 minutes each day to tidying up. Wipe down surfaces, sweep the floor, and put away stray items. These small tasks prevent messes from piling up, making deep cleaning sessions less daunting.

Organizing and decluttering are vital strategies for a serene home. Consider the "one in, one out" rule: for every new item you bring into your home, remove one you no longer need. This practice keeps clutter at bay and forces you to evaluate what truly adds value to your life. Seasonal decluttering sessions are another practical method. As seasons change, go through your belongings and assess their usefulness. Donate clothes you haven't worn in a year, recycle old magazines, and toss expired pantry items. These sessions clear physical space and create mental clarity as you let go of unnecessary burdens.

Efficient cleaning schedules help maintain a clean home without overwhelming you. A weekly cleaning checklist might include vacuuming, dusting, changing bed linens, and cleaning the bathroom. Allocate specific tasks to different days, spreading the workload throughout the week. This approach makes chores more manageable and ensures nothing gets overlooked. For a deeper clean, a monthly plan could cover tasks like washing windows, scrubbing grout, and organizing shelves. Dedicating time to these less frequent tasks prevents dirt and grime from building up, keeping your home fresh year-round.

Visual Element: Sample Weekly Cleaning Schedule

- Monday: Dust surfaces and ceiling fans
- Tuesday: Vacuum all floors and mop or use Swifter
- Wednesday: Clean the bathroom
- Thursday: Change bed linens and do the laundry
- Friday: Organize and declutter one area
- Saturday: Clean the kitchen
- Sunday: Rest and enjoy your clean space

This schedule serves as a flexible guide to help you maintain a tidy home with minimal stress. Adjust it to fit your lifestyle and preferences, ensuring it works for you. Cleaning may not be the most glamorous task, but it's an investment in your well-being. A clean and organized space fosters a sense of control and peace, allowing you to tackle daily challenges with a clear mind. As you embrace these cleaning hacks, you'll find that maintaining a tidy environment becomes second nature, enhancing both your physical health and mental clarity.

With your home in order, the next step is to explore how digital literacy and online safety can further enhance your independent life.

Chapter 6

Digital Literacy and Online Safety

In today's hyper-connected world, your digital footprint is like a shadow that follows you everywhere. Imagine it as a digital breadcrumb trail, left behind by every post, like, and comment you've ever made online. It's a permanent record, indexed by search engines and accessible at the click of a button. Every time you Google your name, you see a reflection of your digital activities. This can include anything from your LinkedIn profile to that old tweet you forgot about. It's easy to overlook the significance of this trail. Still, it's crucial to understand how it shapes your online identity and reputation, both personally and professionally.

Your digital footprint can have a profound impact on your life, influencing how others perceive you. Employers often conduct online searches to vet potential candidates, assessing their suitability for a role. A quick glance at your social media profiles can reveal a lot about your personality, values, and lifestyle. This can work in your favor if your digital presence is polished and professional. However, a single inappropriate post or comment can raise red flags and potentially cost you a job opportunity. Beyond employment, your online reputation affects personal relationships as well. Friends, family, and even romantic interests may form opinions based on what they find about you online. This underscores the importance of managing your digital footprint with care and intention.

Fortunately, there are strategies you can employ to curate a positive online presence. Start by regularly reviewing your privacy settings across all social media platforms. This ensures that you control who sees your information and what they can access. Make it a habit to adjust these settings as platforms update their policies. Alongside this, focus on posting content that reflects positively on you. Share achievements, projects, and insights that highlight your skills and passions. This enhances your professional image and showcases your interests and personality. Remember, every post contributes to your digital narrative, so choose wisely.

When managing your digital footprint, it's also vital to clean up any old, inappropriate posts that could tarnish your reputation. Go through your social media history and delete anything that no longer aligns with your current values or image. This could be an embarrassing photo or a comment made in jest that might be misconstrued. In addition, consider creating a professional online portfolio. This could be a simple blog or website where you showcase your work, skills, and accomplishments. It acts as a controlled environment where you can direct people to see the best of what you have to offer. Such proactive measures help you take charge of your online identity, ensuring that what others find is a reflection of your best self.

Digital Footprint Management Checklist

- Conduct a Search: Google your name to see what comes up. Note any surprises and consider what others might perceive.
- Review Privacy Settings: Regularly check privacy settings on all social media platforms to control who can see your content.
- Curate Content: Post professional and positive content that aligns with your personal and career goals.
- Clean Up: Delete old, inappropriate posts that no longer reflect who you are or want to be.
- Build a Portfolio: Create an online space that showcases your work and achievements to present a polished image.

This checklist can help you manage your digital footprint effectively, ensuring that your online presence supports your ambitions and reflects your true self.

6.1 Data Privacy:

Protecting Your Personal Information

In our digital age, personal data is gold. It's everywhere—embedded in every click, search, and online transaction. But with this digital gold rush comes the looming threat of data breaches and identity theft. Imagine someone gaining unauthorized access to your accounts. The thought alone is unsettling. Hackers can exploit weak security measures, accessing emails, bank accounts, and other sensitive information. This poses a financial risk and jeopardizes your identity. The fallout from a breach can be long-lasting, affecting credit scores and personal reputations. That's why protecting your personal data is not just important; it's imperative.

One of the most practical ways to safeguard your information is by using strong, unique passwords. Think of your password as the key to your digital kingdom. A strong password is complex, mixing upper and lower-case letters, numbers, and symbols. Avoid predictable phrases or sequences. Consider using a password manager to keep track of these complex passwords securely. Another layer of protection is enabling two-factor authentication. This adds an extra step to logging in, usually by sending a code to your mobile device. It might seem like a hassle, but this additional hurdle complicates unauthorized access for potential intruders.

Controlling access to your information extends to your social media and apps as well. Privacy settings on these platforms let you decide who sees your posts and personal details. Regularly review and update these settings to ensure they align with your current preferences. On social media, consider who can view your profile and posts and adjust accordingly. Limiting data sharing across apps is also crucial. Many apps request permission to access various data on your phone, from contacts to location. Be discerning. Only grant permissions necessary for the app's functionality, and periodically review these settings to revoke any that seem excessive or outdated.

Let's look at some real-world applications. On Facebook, for instance, you can adjust privacy settings to control who sees your posts and profile information. Go to settings and privacy to manage who can send you friend requests and see your friends list. On your smartphone, review app permissions by accessing the settings menu. Check which apps can access your location, camera, or contacts, and disable any that don't need it. These steps, although small, create a robust barrier against potential data breaches. They empower you to take control of your digital footprint and protect your personal information from prying eyes.

Data privacy is a dynamic and ongoing process. It's about staying vigilant and regularly updating your practices to keep up with evolving threats. You fortify your digital defenses by employing strong passwords, enabling two-factor authentication, and managing privacy settings. Remember, in a world where information is power, protecting your data means protecting your identity and peace of mind.

6.2 Recognizing and Avoiding Online Scams

Online scams lurk like hidden traps in the digital landscape, ready to ensnare the unwary. These scams come in various forms, each with its unique tactics designed to deceive. Phishing emails, for example, masquerade as legitimate communications from trusted entities. They often contain urgent messages urging you to update your account details or verify personal information. The goal? To trick you into revealing sensitive data. Then there are fake online stores, which entice with unbelievable discounts and offers that seem too good to be true. These sites vanish once payments are made, leaving you empty-handed and out of pocket. Recognizing these scams requires vigilance and a keen eye for detail.

Always verify the source of emails and links to protect yourself from falling victim. If you receive an email from a bank or service provider that seems suspicious, don't click on links or download attachments. Instead, contact the organization directly using verified contact details. Another red flag is the absence of secure website indicators. Legitimate websites use HTTPS, a protocol that ensures data privacy between your browser and the site. Check for a padlock symbol in the address bar before entering sensitive information. This simple step can prevent unauthorized access to your personal data and protect you from potential scams.

Equally important is the act of reporting scams and suspicious activity. By sharing your experiences, you help others avoid similar pitfalls. Contact relevant authorities, such as the Federal Trade Commission, to report scams. Many platforms have dedicated channels for reporting fraudulent activities. Additionally, discussing these encounters with trusted networks can spread awareness and vigilance. For instance, if you identify a phishing attempt in your email, alert your family and friends to be on the lookout for similar messages. This collective effort builds a community of informed individuals who can guard against digital threats.

Consider a scenario where you receive an email from your bank requesting immediate action to secure your account. The email's tone is urgent, and there's a link to a login page. But something feels off. The logo is pixelated, and the sender's address is slightly altered. Trusting your instincts, you contact your bank directly and learn it was a phishing attempt. By not clicking the link, you avoided potential data theft. Or imagine discovering a fraudulent charge on your credit card statement. By promptly disputing it with your bank, not only did you recover your funds, but you also helped track down the scammer. These actions demonstrate the power of awareness and proactive measures in safeguarding against online scams.

6.3 Cybersecurity Basics: Keeping Your Devices Safe

In today's digital landscape, cybersecurity isn't just a buzzword; it's a necessity. Our devices are gateways to vast amounts of personal data, making them prime targets for cyber threats. Malware and viruses are two of the most prevalent dangers lurking online, ready to exploit any vulnerability. Malware, short for malicious software, can infiltrate your system, steal information, and cause irreparable damage. Viruses spread rapidly, corrupting files and compromising device performance. These threats underscore the importance of protecting your devices and data to secure your digital life.

To enhance device security, start with regular software and application updates. These updates often include patches that fix security vulnerabilities, providing an essential layer of protection against new threats. Think of it as keeping your digital armor strong and impenetrable. Set your devices to update automatically or establish a routine to check for updates manually. Next, install reliable antivirus programs to detect and neutralize threats before they cause harm. These programs act as vigilant guards, constantly scanning your system for suspicious activity. Ensure your antivirus software is up-to-date and performs regular scans to maintain optimal protection. This might seem like a basic step, but it's a cornerstone of cybersecurity.

Safe browsing habits are crucial in preventing cyber threats. Avoid visiting suspicious websites or downloading files from unverified sources. These sites often harbor malware, waiting for an unsuspecting click to gain access to your system. Stick to reputable websites and be cautious with downloads, especially those from unfamiliar platforms. Use browser extensions that warn you about unsafe sites and block malicious pop-ups. These tools add an extra layer of security, helping you navigate the internet safely.

Additionally, consider using a Virtual Private Network (VPN) for secure browsing. A VPN encrypts your internet connection, safeguarding your data from prying eyes, especially on public Wi-Fi networks. This encryption ensures that your online activities remain private, protecting sensitive information from potential eavesdroppers.

Imagine browsing online, and a pop-up appears offering a free smartphone. It's tempting, but something feels off. Recognizing malicious pop-ups is essential to avoid falling into traps set by cybercriminals. These pop-ups often contain links to phishing sites or malware downloads. Close them immediately and avoid clicking on any embedded links. Use ad blockers to prevent such pop-ups from appearing in the first place. Another scenario involves using a VPN, which allows you to access your bank account securely while connected to a café's public Wi-Fi. By encrypting your data, the VPN prevents hackers from intercepting sensitive information, ensuring your transactions remain confidential.

Cybersecurity is an ongoing commitment. It's about integrating best practices into your daily digital habits, reinforcing your defenses, and staying informed about emerging threats. By regularly updating your software, installing antivirus programs, practicing safe browsing, and using tools like VPNs, you create a secure environment for your digital activities. These measures protect your devices and data, allowing you to navigate the digital world with confidence and peace of mind. As technology evolves, so will the tactics of cyber threats. Staying vigilant and proactive in your cybersecurity efforts is the key to protecting your digital life.

6.4 Social Media Best Practices:

Sharing Smartly and Safely

Social media is a powerful tool, giving you a platform to express yourself and connect with others. But with great power comes great responsibility. What you share online reflects on you and can impact those around you. It's essential to consider the ripple effect of your posts. Before hitting "share," ask yourself how your content might be received. Could it offend someone? Does it respect the privacy of others? Thinking about these questions ensures that your digital interactions are respectful and considerate. It's easy to overlook the human element in digital spaces, but behind every profile is a real person with feelings and boundaries. Keeping this in mind fosters a more empathetic and understanding online environment.

When engaging on social platforms, it's crucial to practice smart sharing. This means being thoughtful about the information you divulge. Oversharing can inadvertently compromise your privacy. Limit the amount of personal information you post, such as your address or full birthdate, to protect yourself from potential threats.

It's not about being secretive but rather about being selective with what you share. Remember, once something is online, it's challenging to take back. Before posting, pause and reflect on whether the content aligns with your personal and professional image. This practice safeguards your privacy and helps maintain a positive online persona.

Digital citizenship and etiquette are the building blocks of a healthy online community. Engaging constructively and respectfully is vital. Avoiding cyberbullying and harassment should be a given; it's about creating a space where everyone feels safe and respected. Even when opinions differ, engaging in constructive discussions enhances understanding and can lead to insightful exchanges. Respectful debates, where ideas are challenged without personal attacks, enrich the online experience. They foster an environment where diverse perspectives can thrive, contributing to a more thoughtful and inclusive digital space.

Consider the example of curating a professional LinkedIn profile. Think of it as your digital handshake. It's about listing achievements and crafting a narrative that accurately represents your career and aspirations. Highlight your skills, share relevant articles, and engage with content in your field. This builds your network and positions you as a thought leader.

Similarly, participating in positive social media challenges can uplift your profile. Whether it's a book reading challenge or a fitness goal, these activities showcase your interests and commitment. They invite others to join, creating a sense of community and shared purpose. Such practices enhance your personal brand and contribute to a supportive online community, setting a standard for others to follow.

6.5 Digital Well-Being:

Balancing Online and Offline Life

In our fast-paced digital age, the constant pull of screens is hard to ignore. It's easy to get caught up in scrolling through social media, binge-watching shows, or even working late into the night. However, this constant digital consumption can take a toll on our mental and physical health. Excessive screen time can lead to stress and anxiety, as the mind is bombarded with endless information and stimuli. It's like standing in a crowded marketplace, each vendor vying for your attention. This overload can lead to feelings of restlessness and overwhelm. Physically, the effects are just as concerning. Hours spent hunched over devices can contribute to poor posture, leading to back and neck pain. Eye strain is another common issue resulting from staring at screens for extended periods without breaks. This digital fatigue can leave you feeling drained, even if you've been sitting all day.

To maintain digital well-being, it's important to strike a balance between online and offline life. One effective strategy is setting screen time limits. This involves consciously deciding how much time you'll spend on various digital activities each day. Many devices have built-in features that track and limit usage, helping you stay accountable. By setting boundaries, you create more time for other pursuits. Engaging in offline hobbies and activities is a great way to reconnect with the physical world. Whether it's playing a sport, picking up a musical instrument, or simply going for a walk, these activities provide a much-needed mental break and offer a sense of fulfillment that screens can't replicate. They also encourage social interaction, creativity, and physical movement, all of which contribute to a healthier lifestyle.

Mindful technology use is another crucial aspect of digital well-being. This means engaging with technology purposefully rather than mindlessly. Practicing digital mindfulness involves being aware of your digital habits and making intentional choices about when and how you use technology. Start by taking note of how you feel after different digital activities. Do you feel energized after a video call with friends or drained after an hour of social media scrolling? Use this awareness to guide your choices, opting for activities that leave you feeling positive and avoiding those that don't. Consider incorporating mindful breaks into your routine. Take a few minutes to step away from screens, breathe deeply, and refocus your mind. These intentional pauses can help reset your energy and improve your overall digital experience.

Stories of individuals successfully integrating digital and offline life can serve as inspiration. Take Sarah, for example, a busy college student who found herself overwhelmed by the constant demands of digital life. She decided to schedule regular tech-free days, dedicating Sundays to activities like hiking, reading, and spending time with friends. This break allowed her to recharge and return to her studies with renewed focus. Or consider Mark, a young professional who practices mindful media consumption. He limits his news intake to a set time each day and chooses quality over quantity, focusing on trusted sources. This habit keeps him informed without feeling overwhelmed by the constant news cycle. These examples illustrate how small changes can lead to a more balanced and fulfilling life, where digital and offline activities coexist harmoniously.

By understanding these impacts and implementing strategies for balance, you can navigate the digital world more effectively. This chapter has explored how excessive screen time affects well-being and offered practical tips for balancing online and offline life. As you move forward, remember that intentional technology use is key to maintaining your mental and physical health. Embrace the benefits of technology while staying grounded in real-world experiences.

Chapter 7

Building Emotional Intelligence (EI) and Mental Resilience

Imagine you're at a party filled with new faces. As you navigate the room, engaging in conversations, you notice people gravitating towards someone who seems to connect with everyone effortlessly. This person isn't necessarily the loudest or most charismatic. Still, they have an aura of understanding and empathy that draws others in. This magnetic quality is often a reflection of high emotional intelligence (EI). This skill set involves understanding and managing your emotions and those of others. Emotional intelligence is a cornerstone of personal and professional success, acting as a foundation for building and maintaining meaningful relationships.

At its core, emotional intelligence comprises several vital components. Self-awareness is the ability to recognize your emotions as they occur and understand their impact on your thoughts and behavior. It's about knowing your strengths and weaknesses and how they influence your interactions.

Self-regulation Involves:

- Managing your emotions and impulses.
- Staying in control.
- Adapting to changing circumstances without letting emotions dictate your actions.

Motivation, another vital component, drives you to achieve goals with a positive attitude, even in the face of setbacks. It's about channeling emotions to fuel perseverance and enthusiasm. Empathy, the ability to understand and share the feelings of others, allows you to build deeper connections by seeing things from different perspectives. Lastly, social skills enable you to manage relationships effectively, communicate clearly, and build support networks.

In both personal and professional settings, emotional intelligence plays a transformative role. In the workplace, it enhances teamwork and collaboration by fostering an environment where open communication and mutual respect thrive. Colleagues with high EI navigate workplace dynamics smoothly, contributing to a culture of cooperation and understanding. This skill also improves conflict resolution, as individuals can approach disagreements with empathy and composure, leading to constructive solutions rather than escalated tensions. SOURCE 1 highlights that individuals with high EI often excel in their careers as they communicate effectively and manage emotions, leading to improved performance and opportunities for advancement.

Developing emotional intelligence is a journey, not a destination, and there are practical exercises to enhance these skills. Journaling for self-reflection is a powerful tool. By regularly documenting your thoughts and emotions, you gain insight into patterns and triggers, helping you understand your emotional responses. This practice fosters self-awareness and allows you to track your growth over time. Practicing empathy through active listening is another effective exercise. When engaged in conversation, focus intently on the speaker, asking open-ended questions and reflecting back on what you've heard. This validates their feelings and strengthens your ability to connect on a deeper level.

Consider a scenario where a leader uses emotional intelligence to manage team stress effectively. Imagine a project deadline looming with the team feeling overwhelmed. Instead of pushing harder, the leader takes a step back, acknowledging the stress and encouraging open dialogue. They listen to concerns, offering support and guidance. By empathizing and remaining composed, the leader fosters a sense of trust and cooperation, ultimately leading the team to success. Similarly, building rapport with colleagues through empathy can transform workplace relationships. When a teammate shares a personal challenge, showing genuine interest and understanding can create a supportive environment, strengthening bonds and boosting morale.

Interactive Element: Emotional Intelligence Self-Assessment

- Reflect: Take a moment to think about recent interactions at work or in your personal life. How did you handle emotions during these encounters?
- Identify: Write down instances where you demonstrated self-awareness, self-regulation, motivation, empathy, and social skills.
- Evaluate: Consider areas for improvement. Are there situations where you could have been more empathetic or better managed your emotions?
- Plan: Use the strategies discussed and set a goal to enhance one aspect of your emotional intelligence in the coming week.

This self-assessment encourages introspection, guiding you to recognize strengths and opportunities for growth. Emotional intelligence isn't fixed; it's a skill you can nurture and develop over time, leading to richer, more fulfilling experiences in your personal and professional life.

7.1 Stress Management Techniques for Everyday Life

Imagine sitting at your desk, a looming deadline casting a shadow over your day. Emails pile up, each one demanding your attention, while your phone buzzes with messages from friends and family. It's a familiar scene, one where stress creeps in quietly yet persistently. Work deadlines and the pressure to perform can be relentless sources of stress, impacting your mental and physical health. The constant demand to meet expectations can lead to anxiety, insomnia, and even physical ailments like headaches or muscle tension. Personal relationships, too, can be a double-edged sword. While they often provide support and joy, conflicts or misunderstandings can add layers of stress, affecting your emotional well-being.

Recognizing these stressors is the first step toward managing them. Stress triggers vary widely from person to person, making it crucial to identify what specifically causes your stress. Keeping a stress diary can be an effective tool for this. By jotting down situations that cause anxiety, along with your reactions, you can start to see patterns emerge. Perhaps you notice that meetings with a particular colleague leave you feeling drained or that a tight schedule makes you anxious. Understanding these triggers allows you to anticipate and prepare for them, reducing their impact on your health.

With stressors identified, incorporating practical stress management techniques into your routine can make a significant difference. Deep breathing exercises offer a quick and effective way to calm your mind. Focusing on slow, controlled breaths activates your body's relaxation response, slowing your heart rate and reducing tension. This simple practice can be done anywhere, whether at your desk or in traffic, providing instant relief. Progressive muscle relaxation is another technique worth exploring. This involves systematically tensing and then relaxing different muscle groups, helping to release physical tension and promote calmness. By regularly practicing this, you become more attuned to physical stress signals, allowing for earlier intervention.

Time management adjustments can also play a pivotal role in reducing stress. Organizing your tasks and setting realistic deadlines can alleviate the pressure of looming workloads. Prioritize tasks based on urgency and importance and break larger projects into smaller, manageable steps. This clarifies what needs to be done and prevents feeling overwhelmed. Incorporating small breaks throughout your day can also rejuvenate your mind, boost productivity, and reduce stress. A short walk or a few minutes of stretching can clear your head and offer a fresh perspective on tasks.

Real-life examples highlight the effectiveness of these techniques. Consider someone who implements a daily meditation practice to manage stress. Each morning, they dedicate ten minutes to mindfulness meditation, focusing on the present moment and letting go of anxieties about the future. This practice helps them start the day with a clear mind, reducing stress and improving focus. Humor is another powerful stress reducer. You can shift your mindset and release tension by finding light-hearted moments throughout the day, whether through a funny video or a quick chat with a friend. Laughter, after all, is an excellent antidote to stress, triggering the release of endorphins and enhancing your mood.

Stress is inherent in life but doesn't have to dominate yours. By identifying triggers and incorporating effective management techniques, you can navigate daily challenges with greater ease and resilience.

7.2 Building Resilience: Bouncing Back from Setbacks

Imagine the feeling when everything you carefully built seems to crumble in an instant. Life often throws unexpected challenges our way, and resilience is the skill that allows us to adapt and bounce back. It's the ability to recover from setbacks, adapt to change, and keep moving forward, even when the path seems blocked. Whether it's a professional hurdle or a personal crisis, resilience helps you navigate the twists and turns of life. In a world where change is constant, resilience becomes the anchor, providing stability amidst chaos. It's about learning from failures and using them as stepping stones to personal and professional growth.

Developing resilience starts with cultivating a positive outlook. This doesn't mean ignoring difficulties but rather choosing to see challenges as opportunities for growth. When faced with adversity, try to find a silver lining or a lesson to be learned. This perspective shift can foster optimism and empower you to tackle obstacles head-on. Another key strategy is setting realistic goals and expectations. Break larger challenges into smaller, achievable steps. This makes them feel less daunting and allows you to celebrate small victories along the way. These successes build momentum, reinforcing your belief in your ability to overcome difficulties.

Self-compassion plays a crucial role in building resilience. It's about being kind to yourself, especially in moments of failure or disappointment. Practicing self-forgiveness is essential. Recognize that everyone makes mistakes and that these missteps are part of the learning process. Instead of dwelling on what went wrong, focus on what you can do differently next time. This gentle approach to self-reflection can be incredibly healing, allowing you to move forward without the weight of self-criticism holding you back. Embracing this mindset doesn't make challenges disappear but makes them easier to bear.

Consider the story of a professional who unexpectedly lost their job. Initially, the loss felt overwhelming, shattering financial stability and personal identity. However, rather than succumbing to despair, they chose to view this setback as an opportunity to reassess their career goals. By focusing on their strengths and passions, they pursued a new path that aligned more closely with their values. This shift led to personal and professional fulfillment that might not have been possible without the initial challenge. The ability to adapt and find new directions is a testament to the power of resilience.

Another example is someone who faced a relationship setback. The end of a significant relationship left them feeling lost and unsure of their future. Instead of retreating, they embraced self-compassion, allowing themselves time to grieve while also engaging in activities that brought joy and purpose. They connected with friends, pursued new hobbies, and eventually found a renewed sense of self-worth. This personal growth helped them recover and prepared them for healthier, more fulfilling relationships in the future. Such experiences underscore how resilience empowers individuals to transform adversity into a catalyst for growth.

Resilience isn't an innate trait; it's a skill you can cultivate. By developing a positive outlook, setting achievable goals, and practicing self-compassion, you build the strength to face life's challenges with confidence and grace. The stories of those who have rebounded from setbacks illustrate that resilience is not about avoiding difficulties but about meeting them head-on with courage and determination. As you nurture resilience, you'll find that setbacks become less about defeat and more about opportunities for transformation.

7.3 Cultivating a Growth Mindset:

Embracing Challenges

Picture a world where failure isn't the end but a stepping stone to something greater. This is the essence of a growth mindset, a belief that abilities and intelligence can be developed through dedication and hard work. When you view challenges as opportunities, you open yourself up to endless possibilities for learning and development. This mindset transforms obstacles into pathways for growth, encouraging you to embrace effort and persistence as tools for success rather than seeing a roadblock, a puzzle waiting to be solved. This perspective shifts your focus from what you can't do to what you can learn and achieve.

Developing a growth mindset involves shifting your thought patterns from fixed to growth-oriented. It starts with reframing negative thoughts. Instead of thinking, "I'm not good at this," try, "I can improve with practice." This simple change in language alters your approach to challenges, fostering resilience and determination. Seeking feedback is another crucial step. View criticism not as a personal attack but as a valuable source of information that can guide your improvement. This openness to learning from others enhances your skills and broadens your understanding. Embracing feedback is like having a guide on your journey, offering insights and perspectives you might not have considered.

Goal setting plays a pivotal role in cultivating a growth mindset. Setting and achieving goals reinforces the belief that effort leads to progress. SMART goals—Specific, Measurable, Achievable, Relevant, and Time-bound—provide a framework to guide your efforts. Instead of vague aspirations, you create clear targets that direct your energy and focus. For instance, if you're aiming to strengthen your public speaking skills, set a specific goal to deliver a presentation at the next team meeting. Measure your progress by tracking your comfort level and audience feedback. This structured approach enhances your skills and builds confidence and motivation, reinforcing the growth mindset.

Consider the story of an entrepreneur who learned from startup failures. Initially, each setback felt like a personal defeat. However, by adopting a growth mindset, they began to see failures as valuable lessons. Each misstep provided crucial insights into what worked and what didn't. This perspective shift allowed them to refine their strategies, ultimately leading to a successful business venture.

Similarly, a student struggling with grades discovered the power of consistent effort. By focusing on improvement rather than perfection, they steadily raised their grades. Each small victory fueled their motivation, proving that progress is possible with persistence and a willingness to learn.

Adopting a growth mindset transforms how you perceive and tackle challenges. It encourages you to embrace effort as a path to mastery and see failures as opportunities for growth. By reframing negative thoughts, seeking feedback, and setting achievable goals, you develop a mindset that thrives on learning and development. This approach enhances personal and professional growth and fosters a lifelong love of learning and discovery. Embracing a growth mindset is more than just achieving goals; it's about becoming the best version of yourself, constantly evolving, and reaching new heights.

7.4 Establishing a Support Network:

The Power of Community

Imagine navigating through life's ups and downs without a support system. It's like trying to drive a car without fuel; you might move a little, but eventually, you'll stall. Having a solid support network is vital for emotional well-being. It acts as a safety net during difficult times, offering strength and encouragement when you need it most. Emotional support is one of the most significant benefits of a solid network. Whether you're dealing with a breakup, job loss, or any personal crisis, having people to lean on can make all the difference. These connections provide a sense of belonging and reassurance that you're not alone in your struggles. In addition to emotional support, a network offers practical benefits. Friends, family, and colleagues can share resources, offer advice, and help you see situations from different perspectives. This diverse input can be invaluable when making decisions or solving problems.

Building and maintaining a support network requires effort and intentionality. Start by joining community groups or clubs that align with your interests. Whether it's a book club, sports team, or volunteer organization, these settings provide a natural way to meet people and forge connections. Participating in online forums and support groups can also be beneficial, especially if you're looking for specific advice or camaraderie from those with shared experiences. The digital world offers endless possibilities for connection, breaking geographical barriers, and allowing you to interact with people from around the globe. However, it's essential to nurture these connections by being an active participant. Attend meetings regularly, engage in discussions, and show genuine interest in others. Building meaningful relationships takes time, but the rewards are worth the investment.

In a supportive community, the act of giving is just as important as receiving. Offering help to others strengthens bonds and enriches your own life. It could be as simple as lending a listening ear, offering a ride, or sharing a skill. These small acts of kindness foster a sense of reciprocity, creating a community where everyone looks out for each other. Accepting assistance when needed is equally vital. It can be challenging to reach out for help, but doing so fosters trust and deepens relationships. Everyone needs support at various points in life, and being open to receiving it is a sign of strength, not weakness.

Consider the story of a neighborhood group that organized mutual aid during a challenging time. When the pandemic hit, many residents found themselves facing financial struggles and isolation. Recognizing the need, neighbors banded together to create a support network. They coordinated grocery deliveries for those unable to leave their homes, organized virtual social gatherings to combat loneliness, and even established a fund to assist those in financial distress. This initiative provided tangible assistance and strengthened the sense of community, leaving a lasting impact on everyone involved. Similarly, a peer group supporting each other's career advancements can illustrate the power of a supportive network. By sharing job leads, offering feedback on resumes, and celebrating each other's successes, they create an environment where everyone thrives.

Creating a support network is about more than just having people to lean on; it's about building a community that nurtures growth, resilience, and joy. These connections are the threads that weave the fabric of a fulfilling life, offering stability and encouragement through every twist and turn. Embrace the power of community, and you'll find that together, we are stronger, more resilient, and better equipped to face whatever challenges come our way.

7.5 Seeking Professional Help:

When and How to Reach Out

There comes a time when the weight of life's challenges feels too heavy to bear alone. Recognizing this moment is crucial, as it may signal the need for professional support. Many of us experience periods of mental health struggles; they are often marked by persistent feelings of sadness, anxiety, or overwhelming stress. You might notice changes in sleep patterns, a lack of interest in activities you once enjoyed, or difficulty concentrating. These signs indicate that reaching out for professional help could be beneficial. Therapy and counseling offer a safe space to explore these feelings, providing tools to manage emotions and improve mental well-being. Engaging with a mental health professional can be a transformative step, offering clarity and strategies to navigate life's complexities.

Finding the right mental health professional involves some research and consideration. Begin by identifying what you need from therapy. Are you looking for someone to help with anxiety? Or perhaps you're seeking support for relationship issues. Understanding your needs allows you to find a therapist whose specialties align with your goals. Research their credentials, ensuring they are licensed and have relevant experience. Consider exploring different types of therapy, such as Cognitive Behavioral Therapy (CBT), which focuses on changing negative thought patterns, or mindfulness-based therapy, which emphasizes present-moment awareness. Each approach offers unique benefits, and discussing these options with potential therapists can help you choose a method that resonates with you.

Despite the clear benefits of therapy, many people hesitate to seek help due to the stigma surrounding mental health. It's common to fear judgment or worry about appearing weak. However, understanding and addressing these misconceptions is vital.

Sharing personal experiences with trusted friends or family can be a powerful way to break down these barriers. By opening up about your struggles, you create a space for others to share their experiences, fostering mutual support and understanding. Educating yourself and those around you about mental health can also challenge stereotypes, promoting a culture of openness and acceptance. Remember, seeking help isn't a sign of weakness; it's a courageous step toward wellness and growth.

Consider the story of someone who found their way through therapy. Initially hesitant, they decided to seek help after recognizing persistent feelings of anxiety and isolation. Working with a therapist, they explored underlying issues and developed coping strategies. Over time, therapy became a source of strength, offering insights into their emotions and behaviors. This process led to significant personal breakthroughs, strengthening their relationships and overall quality of life. In another example, joining a support group provided a sense of community and shared understanding. Participants found comfort in knowing they weren't alone, gaining confidence and resilience through shared experiences and encouragement.

As we wrap up this chapter, remember that seeking professional help is vital to your mental wellness toolkit. It complements the skills we've discussed, like emotional intelligence and resilience, by providing external support and guidance. Whether through individual therapy or group support, professional intervention can pave the way for profound personal growth and healing. As we move forward, keep these resources in mind and explore how they can enhance your journey toward a balanced and fulfilling life.

Chapter 8

Creating a Fulfilling and Purposeful Life

Imagine waking up each morning with a clear sense of purpose, knowing your day will be filled with activities that align with who you truly are. For many young adults, this vision seems elusive, buried beneath the noise of expectations and societal pressures. Yet, the journey to a fulfilling life often begins with understanding your personal values. These values guide your decisions, relationships, and career paths. They serve as a foundation, offering stability and direction in a world that can often feel chaotic. Without this understanding, you may find yourself drifting, making choices that please others rather than yourself.

Self-reflection is a powerful tool in identifying what truly matters to you. Set aside time to delve into your thoughts and feelings, perhaps through journaling or meditation. Consider questions like, "What makes me feel truly alive?" or "When do I feel most at peace?" These moments of introspection can reveal core values such as integrity, creativity, or compassion. For instance, compassion might be a central value if you find joy in helping others. Understanding these values is not just an academic exercise; it's the key to living authentically and meaningfully. It allows you to align your actions with your beliefs, creating harmony between your inner world and outer experiences.

Values play a critical role in shaping your life choices and goals. They act as a filter through which you can evaluate opportunities and challenges. When faced with a career decision, for example, consider whether the job aligns with your core values. If creativity and innovation are important to you, a position that stifles these may not be fulfilling. Similarly, in relationships, values can guide you in choosing partners who share similar outlooks, fostering deeper connections. By aligning your decisions with your values, you create a life that resonates with who you are rather than what others expect you to be. This alignment fosters a sense of contentment and purpose that is deeply rewarding.

To set meaningful life goals, start by envisioning your future. What do you want to achieve? What legacy do you wish to leave? Creating a vision board can be an effective way to visualize these aspirations. Collect images, words, and symbols that represent your dreams and arrange them on a board. Display it prominently as a constant reminder of your goals. Writing a personal mission statement is another powerful exercise. This statement should encapsulate your core values and long-term objectives, serving as a guiding light in your decision-making process. A clear mission statement clarifies your intentions and motivates you to pursue them with vigor and determination.

Consider the story of a young woman passionate about social justice. She realized early on that her values of equality and fairness were non-negotiable. These values led her to pursue a career in law, focusing on human rights advocacy. Her career choice wasn't just about a job but about living her values and making a difference in the world. Similarly, a young man deeply committed to environmental conservation chose to live in a community that prioritized sustainability. This decision aligned with his values, allowing him to contribute to initiatives that reduced the community's carbon footprint. These examples illustrate how values-driven decisions can lead to fulfilling and impactful life choices.

Reflection Exercise: Identifying Your Core Values

1. Set Aside Quiet Time: Find a peaceful space where you won't be disturbed.
2. Reflect on Key Questions: Consider what activities bring you joy and fulfillment. What principles are non-negotiable in your life?
3. Journaling: Write down words or phrases that resonate with your sense of self. Don't overthink; let your thoughts flow.
4. Identify Patterns: Look for recurring themes in your responses. Are there values that consistently appear?
5. Prioritize: Choose the top three to five values that feel most integral to your identity.

By engaging in this exercise, you pave the way for a life that is not only fulfilling but also true to who you are at your core.

8.1 Pursuing Passions and Hobbies:

Enriching Your Life

Imagine a Saturday afternoon where you lose track of time, not because you're working late or stuck on chores, but because you're completely absorbed in something you love. This is the beauty of pursuing passions and hobbies. Engaging in activities outside of work is more than just a way to pass the time—it's a vital part of personal fulfillment. By immersing yourself in hobbies, whether it's painting, hiking, or playing music, you create a space where stress melts away. Creative outlets like these offer a respite from daily pressures, allowing your mind to wander freely and recharge. Studies have shown that engaging in enjoyable activities can significantly reduce stress, leading to a greater sense of well-being and satisfaction with life (SOURCE 2).

Discovering and nurturing these passions might seem daunting, especially with so many options available. Start by exploring different avenues—sign up for a local class or workshop in something that piques your interest. If you've always been curious about photography, enroll in a beginner's course. This provides foundational skills and connects you with others who share your interests. Setting aside dedicated time for hobbies is equally important. Life gets busy, and it's easy to let these interests fall by the wayside. Schedule regular blocks of time in your calendar to focus solely on your hobby. Treat it as an appointment with yourself that's just as important as any work meeting. This consistency helps deepen your engagement and allows your skills to flourish over time.

Pursuing diverse interests enriches your personal life and contributes to a well-rounded existence. By exploring various hobbies, you build a repertoire of skills and knowledge that can open unexpected doors. For instance, learning to cook can improve your health and save money, while learning a new language might enhance travel experiences or career opportunities. These activities also introduce you to communities of like-minded individuals. Participating in a book club or a sports team fosters new friendships and expands your social network. The shared passion creates a bond that transcends other differences, providing a sense of belonging and shared purpose.

Consider the story of a friend who took up photography as a hobby. What started as a casual interest soon became a passion. They developed a professional portfolio by dedicating time each week to practice and explore different techniques. This opened up freelance work and exhibition opportunities, transforming a simple pastime into a fulfilling career path. Then, there's another acquaintance who picked up knitting as a way to unwind. Through online forums and local meet-ups, this hobby blossomed into a vibrant community project where knitters came together to create blankets for charity. Not only did this enhance their skills, but it also brought joy and purpose through giving back.

Having passions and hobbies enriches life in ways that extend far beyond the activities themselves. They provide a sense of identity and accomplishment that can be profoundly rewarding. Whether discovering a new interest or nurturing an existing one, these pursuits add color and depth to everyday life. They remind you there's more to living than work and obligations, offering a playground for creativity and self-discovery. As you explore these interests, you'll find that they enhance your well-being and provide a foundation for personal growth and fulfillment.

8.2 Sustainable Living: Making Eco-Friendly Choices

Picture a world where every small action you take contributes to a healthier planet. This is the essence of sustainable living, a lifestyle choice that prioritizes the well-being of our environment. The urgency of environmental sustainability is clear, and as young adults, you hold the power to lead the charge toward a more eco-friendly future. By reducing your carbon footprint, you're protecting natural resources and ensuring a better quality of life for generations to come. Choosing sustainability means supporting ethical consumption, where the products you buy align with values of fairness and environmental care. It's about making informed choices that serve individual and collective needs, creating a ripple effect of positive change across the globe.

Incorporating sustainability into your daily life doesn't mean overhauling your entire routine overnight. Instead, focus on practical, actionable steps that can seamlessly fit into your lifestyle. Start by swapping single-use items for reusable alternatives. Consider carrying a metal water bottle instead of buying plastic bottles or using cloth bags for shopping. These small changes reduce waste and decrease your environmental impact. Transportation is another area where you can make a significant difference. Opting for public transportation, biking, or carpooling reduces emissions and often saves money. By choosing these modes of transport, you're contributing to cleaner air and conserving energy, supporting the planet's health while improving your own.

The benefits of sustainable living extend beyond environmental impact; they also enhance personal well-being. Making eco-friendly choices often means reducing exposure to harmful chemicals found in many conventional products. For example, using natural cleaning supplies minimizes chemical exposure and protects indoor air quality. Additionally, energy-efficient practices, like using LED lights or unplugging devices when not in use, can lead to significant savings on utility bills. These practices demonstrate how sustainability can be practical and economical, offering benefits that improve your quality of life while supporting the planet.

Consider the story of a family who decided to reduce their household waste through composting. They set up a compost bin in their backyard and began collecting kitchen scraps and yard waste. Over time, they noticed a reduction in their garbage output and a healthier garden enriched by the nutrient-rich compost. This small change minimized landfill contributions and fostered a deeper connection with their food and environment. Another individual, motivated by environmental concerns, transitioned to a plant-based diet. This shift reduced their carbon footprint and improved their health, leading to more energy and a greater sense of well-being. These examples illustrate how adopting sustainable practices can lead to tangible, positive outcomes in everyday life.

Interactive Element: Eco-Friendly Challenge

- Week 1: Replace single-use plastics with reusable alternatives.
- Week 2: Incorporate one plant-based meal per day.
- Week 3: Use public transportation or carpool twice a week.
- Week 4: Conduct an energy audit of your home and implement one energy-saving measure.

Participating in this challenge offers a structured approach to integrating eco-friendly habits into your life. These steps contribute to a healthier planet and cultivate a more conscious, intentional lifestyle. Sustainable living isn't about perfection; it's about progress and making choices that reflect a commitment to the future. No matter how small, each action plays a part in shaping a more sustainable world.

8.3 Volunteering and Giving Back:

Creating Impactful Change

Imagine walking into a community center bustling with energy, where people from all walks of life gather to make a positive impact. Volunteering offers this unique opportunity to step outside your daily routine and engage with the world in a meaningful way. It's about more than just giving your time; it's about fostering a sense of empathy and understanding. When you volunteer, you open yourself up to new experiences and perspectives, learning to see the world through the eyes of others. This growth in empathy can enrich your interactions, making you more compassionate and aware of the diverse challenges people face in different circumstances.

Finding the right volunteer opportunity starts with aligning your efforts with causes that resonate with your personal values. Begin by researching local organizations and initiatives that align with issues you care about. If education is your passion, look for mentoring programs where you can share your knowledge and help guide students toward success. If the environment speaks to you, join community cleanup efforts or conservation projects. Identifying the skills you can offer is also crucial. Whether it's tutoring, organizing events, or providing technical expertise, your unique talents can make a significant impact. Reach out to organizations directly or explore platforms connecting volunteers with opportunities, ensuring your contributions are meaningful and impactful.

The benefits of volunteering extend far beyond the immediate impact of your actions. It provides a profound sense of purpose, contributing to personal well-being and community health. Acts of service strengthen community bonds, creating a network of support and collaboration. These connections enhance community resilience and offer you a sense of belonging and fulfillment. By working together toward common goals, you gain new perspectives and experiences that can enrich your life. Volunteering exposes you to diverse viewpoints and challenges, fostering personal growth and a more profound understanding of societal issues.

Consider the story of a college student who volunteered in a mentoring program for underprivileged youth. Through weekly sessions, they helped students with their studies and inspired them to dream bigger. Over time, the student's academic performance and self-confidence improved significantly, leading to educational success and life-changing opportunities. Another example is a local community that organized regular cleanup initiatives to improve their neighborhood. By banding together, they transformed neglected parks into vibrant spaces, fostering a sense of pride and community ownership. These stories illustrate the lasting positive effects that volunteering can have, both for the individuals involved and the wider community.

Volunteering is not just an activity but a pathway to creating impactful change. By offering your time and skills, you contribute to a collective effort that can transform communities and enrich your life in unexpected ways. Each experience builds a bridge between you and the world, fostering growth, empathy, and understanding.

8.4 Maintaining Healthy Relationships:

Communication and Boundaries

Healthy relationships are a cornerstone of a fulfilling life, providing the emotional support and companionship that enrich our everyday experiences. They are the ties that hold us steady when the world feels uncertain, offering a sanctuary where we can be vulnerable yet feel safe. Positive connections with friends, family, and partners contribute significantly to our overall well-being, enhancing happiness and reducing stress. When you have people you can rely on, the weight of life's challenges becomes lighter, and the joys become more profound. These relationships are built on mutual trust, understanding, and the ability to communicate openly.

Effective communication is the lifeblood of any healthy relationship. It involves more than just exchanging words—it's about truly listening and understanding. Active listening is a skill that requires your full attention, showing the other person that their thoughts and feelings matter. When a friend shares their struggles, listen with empathy and resist the urge to offer immediate solutions. Instead, acknowledge their feelings and offer support. Expressing your own needs and feelings is equally important. Instead of bottling up emotions, articulate them honestly and respectfully. Saying, "I feel overwhelmed when our plans change at the last minute," opens a dialogue and helps prevent misunderstandings.

Setting and respecting boundaries is vital in maintaining balance and respect in relationships. Boundaries are the invisible lines that protect your well-being, defining what you are comfortable with and what you are not. They are not about creating distance but about maintaining a healthy space for yourself within a relationship. Identifying your personal limits is the first step. Reflect on situations where you feel uncomfortable or resentful, which may indicate areas where boundaries are needed. Once you recognize these limits, communicate them assertively. Use "I" statements to express your needs without blaming others. For instance, "I need some quiet time after work to recharge" is a clear way to set a boundary with roommates or family.

Consider the story of two friends who managed to strengthen their relationship through mutual respect and understanding. They found themselves drifting apart due to miscommunications and unmet expectations. Instead of letting resentment build, they decided to have an open conversation about their needs and boundaries. By actively listening to each other and expressing their feelings honestly, they were able to rebuild their friendship on a foundation of trust and respect. Another example involves navigating family dynamics with clear boundaries. A young adult living at home found it challenging to establish independence. By setting boundaries around personal time, they could create a more harmonious living situation, enhancing both their autonomy and family relationships.

Healthy relationships require effort but offer immense rewards. They are about finding that delicate balance between expressing yourself and respecting the other person. Through effective communication and boundary-setting, you can maintain supportive, enriching, and resilient relationships. As you nurture these connections, you'll find that they enhance your personal life and empower you to face life's challenges with confidence and grace.

8.5 Embracing Change and Uncertainty with Confidence

Change is as certain as the sunrise, yet it often arrives unannounced, shaking the foundation of what we know. While it can be unsettling, embracing change can lead to profound personal growth and resilience. Change acts as a catalyst for transformation, pushing us out of our comfort zones and into new realms of possibility. This process, although challenging, often opens the door to opportunities that would otherwise remain hidden. When you view change as a positive force, you shift your mindset from resistance to acceptance, allowing yourself to adapt and thrive. The key to harnessing this potential lies in your ability to embrace uncertainty with an open heart.

Developing flexibility and open-mindedness is crucial when navigating life's unpredictability. These traits enable you to adjust your sails rather than fight the wind, making the most of whatever comes your way. One practical strategy is to practice mindfulness, which keeps you anchored in the present moment. Focusing on the here and now reduces anxiety about the future, allowing you to respond to change with clarity and calmness. Staying present involves paying attention to your thoughts and surroundings without judgment, which can be achieved through meditation or simple breathing exercises. This approach enhances mental clarity and fosters a sense of inner peace, equipping you to confidently handle life's surprises.

Maintaining a positive outlook during transitions can significantly influence how you experience and adapt to change. Optimism serves as a buffer against stress, encouraging you to see potential benefits even in uncertain situations. By focusing on the positives, you cultivate a mindset open to learning and growth. Building a support network is also vital, as it provides encouragement and perspective when faced with challenges. Surround yourself with people who uplift and inspire you, offering advice and support when you need it most. These connections act as a safety net, reminding you that you're not alone on this journey and that you can overcome any obstacle together.

Consider the story of a young professional who faced an unexpected career shift. Initially daunting, this change eventually led to a role more aligned with personal passions and strengths. By approaching the transition with curiosity and an open mind, this individual discovered new skills and interests that had previously been unexplored. Similarly, embracing a new cultural environment can offer rich experiences and insights. A friend who moved abroad for work found the initial uncertainty overwhelming. However, by engaging with the local community and embracing cultural differences, they developed a deeper appreciation for diversity and personal growth. These stories illustrate how embracing change can lead to fulfilling personal and professional transformations, expanding your horizons in ways you never imagined.

As you navigate life's ever-changing landscape, remember that each moment of uncertainty holds the potential for growth and discovery. Embracing change with an open heart allows you to transform challenges into opportunities, building resilience and strength along the way. Transitioning into new chapters of life with optimism and support can lead to profound personal growth and fulfillment. As we move forward, we'll explore how these principles apply to embracing the future with a sense of adventure and purpose.

CONCLUSION

As you stand on the cusp of adulthood, this book has aimed to be your companion, offering guidance and support through the many facets of this transformative journey. We've traveled together through the intricacies of financial responsibility, beginning with the essential skills of budgeting and understanding credit. These tools are the foundation of financial independence, enabling you to navigate life's complexities with confidence and foresight.

In our exploration of communication, we've uncovered the importance of mastering professional emails, active listening, and conflict resolution. These skills are not just about exchanging information; they are about building meaningful connections and fostering understanding in both personal and professional settings. Whether crafting a resume or preparing for an interview, these communication skills will serve as your anchors in the competitive world of work.

Navigating workplace dynamics demands resilience and adaptability, and we've delved into strategies to manage these challenges effectively. From crafting standout resumes to understanding employment benefits, each insight is designed to empower you in your career pursuits. As you balance these professional demands, the importance of time management, self-care, and maintaining a work-life balance cannot be overstated. You create space for personal growth and fulfillment by prioritizing tasks and setting boundaries.

Safeguarding your online presence is paramount in the digital age. We've discussed managing your digital footprint, enhancing cybersecurity, and practicing mindful social media engagement. These practices protect your personal information and shape your reputation in the digital world.

Emotional intelligence and mental resilience form the bedrock of personal growth. By cultivating these skills, you enhance your ability to connect with others and navigate life's challenges with grace. From stress management techniques to building a supportive community, these strategies reinforce your inner strength and adaptability.

Creating a fulfilling life involves aligning your actions with your values and passions. We've explored the significance of pursuing hobbies, making eco-friendly choices, and volunteering to effect positive change. These pursuits enrich your life, offering joy, purpose, and a sense of belonging.

The insights we've gathered on this journey are numerous and varied. By putting into practice what you've learned, you are set to manage your finances astutely, communicate with impact, and excel in your career. Equipped with the tools for effective time management, digital safety, and emotional resilience, you're prepared to forge a life that mirrors your deepest values and ambitions, promoting personal growth and a positive impact on those around you. By applying the lessons learned, you can become financially savvy, communicate effectively, and thrive in professional settings. You'll be equipped to manage your time, protect your digital identity, and nurture your emotional well-being. Most importantly, you'll build a life that reflects your values and aspirations, fostering personal and collective growth.

This book's vision has always been to serve as a practical and relatable guide for young adults like you. As you transition into independence, remember that these skills and strategies are your toolkit for navigating adulthood's complexities. Embrace them, experiment with them, and let them guide you toward a balanced and successful life.

I encourage you to actively implement these insights into your daily routine. Start small, with a single habit or change, and gradually expand your efforts. Whether setting a budget, practicing active listening, or exploring a new hobby, each step brings you closer to the life you envision.

Thank you for allowing me to accompany you on this journey. Your engagement and dedication to self-improvement are genuinely inspiring. Remember, adulthood is not a destination but a continuous journey of learning and growth. As you move forward, carry these lessons with you, confident in your ability to create a life that is not only successful but also deeply satisfying.

SCAN ME & LEAVE A REVIEW

REFERENCES

- *Best Budgeting Apps Of October 2024* https://www.forbes.com/advisor/banking/best-budgeting-apps/
- *How Gen Z and Millennials Can Improve Their Credit* https://www.cnbc.com/select/how-gen-z-and-millennials-can-improve-their-credit/
- *Debt Consolidation Strategies for Millennials to Pay Off Debt* https://alleviatefinancial.com/debt-settlement/debt-consolidation-strategies-for-millennials/
- *Best High-Yield Savings Accounts Of October 2024* https://www.forbes.com/advisor/banking/savings/best-high-yield-savings-accounts/
- *Why Professional Email Etiquette is Important* https://www.hurleywrite.com/blog/writing-skills/why-is-email-etiquette-important-in-the-workplace/
- *7 Active Listening Techniques For Better Communication* https://www.verywellmind.com/what-is-active-listening-3024343
- *Navigating Conflict in the Workplace: A Guide for Young ...* https://www.linkedin.com/pulse/navigating-conflict-workplace-guide-young-employees-l-k-monu-borkala-wrooc
- *Your Social Media Presence Can Help You Land (or Lose) ...* https://hbr.org/2024/05/your-social-media-presence-can-help-you-land-or-lose-a-job-opportunity
- *How To Write Cover Letters That Stand Out (With example)* https://www.indeed.com/career-advice/resumes-cover-letters/cover-letters-that-stand-out
- *Young Professionals Guide to Interview Prep* https://www.linkedin.com/pulse/young-professionals-guide-interview-prep-matthew-mulhern
- *5 Secrets To A LinkedIn Profile That Can Compete In The ...* https://www.forbes.com/sites/ashleystahl/2023/01/09/5-

secrets-to-a-linkedin-profile-that-can-compete-in-the-2023-job-market/
- *Workplace Dynamics: Navigating Office Politics with Integrity* https://www.linkedin.com/pulse/workplace-dynamics-navigating-office-politics-integrity-arcaligned-hrque
- *How to be More Productive by Using the "Eisenhower Box"* https://jamesclear.com/eisenhower-box
- *5 Ways To Set Incredible Boundaries Like Gen Z* https://www.ivyhouse.co.uk/news-views/articles/5-ways-to-set-incredible-boundaries-like-gen-z/
- *5 Steps to Creating a Personalized Scheduling Template* https://doodle.com/en/5-steps-to-creating-a-personalized-scheduling-template/
- *The Effectiveness of Mindfulness-Based Stress Reduction ...* https://www.ncbi.nlm.nih.gov/pmc/articles/PMC7511255/
- *22 Cheap and Easy Meals for College Students* https://www.allrecipes.com/gallery/cheap-and-easy-meals-for-college-students/
- *10 Tips for Planning Meals on a Budget* https://www.unlockfood.ca/en/Articles/Budget/10-Tips-for-Planning-Meals-on-a-Budget.aspx
- *How to Understand and Use the Nutrition Facts Label* https://www.fda.gov/food/nutrition-facts-label/how-understand-and-use-nutrition-facts-label
- *15 Basic Home Repair and Maintenance Skills You Should ...* https://www.windowworldstlouis.com/blog/basic-home-repair-skills
- *Advice for Teens: Manage Your Digital Footprint* https://maryandersonline.umd.edu/resources/advice-teens-manage-your-digital-footprint
- *What Is Digital Privacy and Its Importance?* https://digitalprivacy.ieee.org/publications/topics/what-is-digital-privacy-and-its-importance

- *Top 9 Most Common Online Scams and How to Avoid Them* https://www.pnc.com/insights/personal-finance/protect/top-online-scams-how-to-avoid.html
- *6 tips Gen Z need to know about cybersecurity* https://www.techradar.com/vpn/6-tips-gen-z-need-to-know-about-cybersecurity
- *The Importance Of Emotional Intelligence At Work* https://www.forbes.com/councils/forbeshumanresourcescouncil/2023/07/18/the-importance-of-emotional-intelligence-at-work/
- *18 Effective Stress Relief Strategies* https://www.verywellmind.com/tips-to-reduce-stress-3145195
- *Resilience: Build skills to endure hardship* https://www.mayoclinic.org/tests-procedures/resilience-training/in-depth/resilience/art-20046311
- *Dweck's Fixed and Growth Mindsets* https://www.mindtools.com/asbakxx/dwecks-fixed-and-growth-mindsets
- *Values-Guided Career Searching* https://www.ncda.org/aws/NCDA/pt/sd/news_article/459878/_PARENT/CC_layout_details/false
- *How Hobbies Improve Mental Health* https://extension.usu.edu/mentalhealth/articles/how-hobbies-improve-mental-health
- *Sustainable Living for Young Adults: How to Embrace ...* https://www.elephantjournal.com/2024/03/sustainable-living-for-young-adults-how-to-embrace-environmental-consciousness-in-your-20s-madeline-lillis/
- *Generation Z and Perspectives on Volunteering* https://www.jaaz.org/generation-z-and-perspectives-on-volunteering/

Made in the USA
Monee, IL
15 January 2025